the CATCH

SEA-TO-TABLE RECIPES, STORIES & SECRETS

BEN SARGENT

with **PETER KAMINSKY**

Photographs by Gabriela Herman

CLARKSON POTTER/PUBLISHERS
NEW YORK

All photographs are by Gabriela Herman with the exception of those on pp. 4–5,
9–11, 22, 105, 118, 141, 148, 232 (courtesy of the author); p. 14, bottom (by Jane
Borock); p. 17 (by Beowulf Sheehan; p. 30 (by Ethan Daniels); pp. 73, 208 (by
Annica Lydenberg); p. 194 (by Daniel Gritzer); and pp. 224–25 (by Cody Raisig).

Cooking Channel photographs (pp. 30, 39, 50, 52, 62, 74, 80, 88, 126, 132, 151,
162, 170, 176, 203, 209, 211, 229) are provided courtesy of Cooking Channel, LLC.
© 2012 Cooking Channel, LLC.

Library of Congress Cataloging-in-Publication Data
Sargent, Ben, 1977–
    The catch : sea-to-table recipes, stories & secrets / Ben Sargent with Peter
Kaminsky ; photographs by Gabriela Herman.
        pages cm
1. Cooking (Seafood)   2. Sargent, Ben, 1977—Travel.
I. Kaminsky, Peter. II. Title.
    TX747.S285 2013
    641.6'92—dc23   2012050245

ISBN 978-0-307-98552-1
eISBN 978-0-307-98553-8

Printed in the United States of America

Book and cover design by Dirty Bandits
Cover photographs by Gabriela Herman

10 9 8 7 6 5 4 3 2 1

First Edition

This book is dedicated to my mom, who
always made our kitchen a warm and cozy
place. As a single mom for a long time,
she was a real good sport about cooking
the fish I brought home as a kid. She
was a huge inspiration as she lived with
breast cancer for such a long time.

This book is for her in so many ways.

CONTENTS

INTRODUCTION

UNCHOWDERED TERRITORIES

In kindergarten, my love of eating fish earned me a trip to the principal's office. I wasn't sure why I had been called in or why my mom was there. "Do you realize your son has been eating live minnows on class trips?" the principal asked. My parents thought it was great that I (a) knew how to catch them and (b) knew how to eat them! My mom didn't look fazed. She turned to the principal. "Yeah, he does that all the time. And I'm afraid we actually taught him how to do that."

In my early years, one of my favorite places was my grandfather's bait and tackle store, the Goose Hummock Shop, on Pleasant Bay, Cape Cod. We had a family summer house and there was a wing with a bedroom that became mine during the fishing season. I loved the musty, briny, seaweed smell. The "decor" was a lobster shell, a blowfish, and family sketches and seascapes that my grandmother drew when she wasn't fishing and hunting.

My grandfather wasn't a chef, but he understood cooking, like how to make a really nice broth or a proper chowdah. After a full day of fishing, my grandfather, Pup, would always dig a few clams on the way back to the house. Then he'd rip through a flounder in one cut, like one of the mates on the charter boats. He'd miss some meat that way, but we caught enough fish back then that it didn't matter. The heads and bones and tails went into the stockpot and became the soul of the chowder.

His chowders were perfect. Often, he would do a New England clam chowder. One giant quahog—the local name for a large hard-shell clam—then cream, potatoes, dill, and butter. He also did a seafood chowder, where he'd throw in razor clams, steamers, quahogs, conch, striper, and potatoes. Anything caught that day went in the chowder. His cooking inspired me. Now when I find an authentic New England clam chowder, I'll say, "Yep, this is how Pup made it." That's the highest compliment I can give. Not too thick, and brimming with flavor.

My grandfather wasn't a chef, but he understood cooking, like how to make a really nice broth or a proper chowdah.

9

If Pup gave me my love of fishing and Mom passed on her sense of food, my true appreciation of the sea came from my dad, Bill Sargent.

Pup's chowders were the best, but my true love of cooking came from my mom. She was a natural cook who didn't worry all that much about following recipes. When I picture her, I see her behind the stove in an apron and ski boots, ordering my poor stepdad, Paul, around the kitchen. I get my love of heavy cream and butter from my mom. She could go through an entire box of breadsticks dipping each bite into a stick of butter. Modern health warnings were not at the top of my mom's list of worries; she would eat raw hamburger meat right out of the package. She made the kitchen the center of our home, and she had an obsession with Italian food. Even though she was the daughter of two Jewish immigrants from Germany, I didn't see a German or Jewish dish come out of her kitchen, aside from the occasional brisket or potato pancake. Everything else was Italian and all of it was amazing.

If Pup gave me my love of fishing and Mom passed on her sense of food, my true appreciation of the sea came from my dad, Bill Sargent. He is a naturalist in the great New England tradition. He notices every little thing in nature—from an ant crossing the path, to the Indian shells on the side of the bank, or a crab eating a minnow. On any given afternoon, he would give me a history lesson, taking me back a few million years just by pointing out the rocks, eroding bluffs, and a horseshoe crab scooting along the shallows. His endless notes about horseshoe crabs and salt marshes only begin to tell the tale of his fascination with sea life.

SURF DAYS

Throughout my childhood and teenage years, I got my surfing practice on Cape Cod. We surfers look for hurricanes. I don't mean that we go out in eighty-mile-an-hour winds. But when a hurricane forms farther south in the Atlantic, it sets up big waves, which make for great surfing by the time they hit the Cape. My friends and I constantly listened to the radio for updates, trying to figure out when the swell would arrive. No sooner did we get news of waves than we'd grab our boards and paddle out. Often we'd take a real beating, but it was worth it! We were hopeful.

My friends and I constantly listened to the radio for updates, trying to figure out when the swell would arrive. No sooner did we get news of waves than we'd grab our boards and paddle out. Often we'd take a real beating, but it was worth it!

So hopeful that I took the Internet handle Hurricane Hopeful. A few years later, when I moved to Brooklyn and opened a chowder bar, I called it Hurricane Hopeful. But this was before we knew about Katrina and Sandy.

While I was getting my surfing life together, I worked in an ice cream shop in Wellfleet. Behind the shop was a place called Mac's Fish where locals worked. They were a bunch of hooligans, but they got the job that I wanted but couldn't have because I wasn't a local. It didn't matter that I spent all summer, every summer on Cape Cod; the fact that our winter home was in Cambridge, Mass., made me an outsider. I envied the Wellfleet fish kids. I thought everything about them was cool: They carried knives, they called out chowder orders in real Cape Cod accents. They never let me near the fish, because handling fish was reserved for Cape Codders. The aroma filled up the pier and I couldn't resist the food those kids cooked up. It was delicious, and it shaped me.

One day, I saw a guy walk by the window with a surfboard. I couldn't believe it and ran out and asked him where he could possibly be going with a surfboard. "To the Rockaways."

BIG APPLE, BIG WAVES

My next stop was in a seemingly unlikely place for a surfer and fisherman: Brooklyn. It didn't start well. In 2001, as I went to get the keys for my first apartment, I met the broker on the sidewalk. She opened the door and there on the floor lay the previous tenant. He appeared to have passed out after rolling off his couch with a bottle of vodka in his hand. Being a friendly kind of guy, I went over to help him up off the floor. His hand was freezing cold. The broker asked, "Is he okay?" "No, I think he's dead," I said.

I took a late-night job delivering food in Bushwick. In 2001, this was not a good 'hood at four o'clock in the morning. I walked away from that and looked after a small gift shop that my friends, soap stars from *As the World Turns*, owned in Williamsburg, Brooklyn. Then, one day, I saw a guy walk by the window with a surfboard. I couldn't believe it and ran out and asked him where he could possibly be going with a surfboard. "To the Rockaways."

I locked up the shop and jumped on the L train with a fellow surfer (named Luke), and we went out to the Rockaways, where he had a bungalow.

We got off at the Eighty-eighth Street stop in Queens. Luke showed me his surf shack, and the next thing I knew, I was suited up in his hand-me-down gear and we were surfing. Walking over the boardwalk with the sun low in the sky and seeing a peeling barreling left—that is, a really good surfing wave—was something my Cape Cod brain could not wrap itself around. I was forty-five minutes from Brooklyn. It seemed impossible. But there it was. Within a month, I opened my own surf shop in Williamsburg, Brooklyn.

Business was slow, so I served chowder to attract clientele. It was Sarge's Chowder, based on my grandfather's recipe. I made it right there on the candle-making stove from the former gift shop!

The next thing I knew, I was suited up in his hand-me-down gear and we were surfing . . . I was 45 minutes from Brooklyn. It seemed impossible, but there it was.

BROOKLYN'S BOUNTIFUL WAVES

Perhaps the most surprising thing about my life in New York City wasn't the surfing, or the way I could re-create a version of Pup's fishing garage in my little New York apartment and business. It was that I could fish in the East River, which was out my back door!

There are lots of fish here! And they're not radioactive. I discovered this when I wandered over to the water just a few blocks from my house to test out a new rod. I was going to Cape Cod for the weekend and decided to try a cast while standing on a graffiti-covered concrete slab. No sooner did I start retrieving my first cast than BAM! A bluefish nailed the little rubber shad and leaped clear out of the water! I now fish the East River consistently for stripers and blues with views of the Manhattan skyline right smack in front of me.

One day, I got the idea to start a Brooklyn fishing competition: an East River Derby. I didn't think many people would sign up, and I was sure the few who did would only be in it for the cool T-shirt. But people signed up left and right: There were all types of fishermen representing Brooklyn! We had graphic designers and fashion stylists who had grown up fishing farm ponds in the Midwest. We got Polish guys who worked on the high-rises going up on the waterfront, Italian guys who'd fished there their whole lives, Jamaican guys, Dominican guys. They all took the derby seriously. And to this day, we fish all of October and we fish hard! The biggest fish that first year was caught by Jan Gorz, and it was forty-six inches! For those of you not in the know about striped bass fishing, that is one big urban fish!

A few years later I came up with the idea of making and selling lobster rolls in my apartment. I had been out of restaurants for a while and I felt that New York lobster-roll makers were pretty clueless. They spent their efforts decorating, garnishing, fancifying, and—in my mind—messing up a good lobster roll.

No sooner did I start retrieving my first cast than BAM! A bluefish nailed the little rubber shad and leaped clear out of the water!

Pretty soon, I couldn't keep up with the lobster roll demand. I'd make a hundred fifty lobster rolls on a good day.

Pretty soon, I couldn't keep up with the lobster roll demand. I'd make a hundred fifty lobster rolls on a good day, which made my suppliers in Maine very happy, but there were times when I was on the verge of tears because I couldn't make them fast enough. By then, the New York City Fire Department had caught wind of the operation and come by to check out my setup, which was absolutely and completely illegal because I had enough propane in my apartment to blow up the entire building. Hmm . . . what to do?

"Do you guys like lobster?" I asked.

"Yeah, we do. We like lobstah," the chorus of firefighters agreed, in their Brooklyn accents.

"Let's strike a deal. I'll get this place cleaned up as fast as I know how, and you don't tell your fire chief how bad it was when you first got down here, and you can feel free to stop by for lobster rolls any time you want." By the time the chief got there, the place was cleaned up and the propane was one hundred yards from the house in the neighbors' garden.

Nevertheless, the chief walked me around the block and gave me a few words of advice: "Mr. Sargent, do me a fayvah. Get a real f*****g job."

I thought for sure I was finished when the fire department notified my landlord, Frank. But Frank was cool enough to let me keep cooking down there. He just didn't want me selling out of my apartment, now known as the "Underground Lobster Pound." So people would call in their orders and I would deliver the lobster rolls on the street. Then one night, a strange, and for me, lucky, thing happened. A kid came by to pick up an order that he had phoned in. I went out to meet him carrying his order in a brown paper bag. He had his money rolled up in his hand and gave me a quick handshake along with the money. I handed him the bag, and off he went into the night. We never spoke a word.

A lightbulb went off in my head. Where had I seen this movie before? The anonymous phone call. The handshake, the handover. My Dr. Klaw persona

My Dr. Klaw persona wore a red jumpsuit with a huge gold claw when making exchanges on the street.

wore a red jumpsuit with a huge gold claw. I would look in the mirror and even surprise myself. At fourteen dollars a pop, everyone would tip six dollars because Dr. Klaw wasn't gonna make change for them in the street!

When I took my rolls of cash to the bank, the teller said, "Is it appropriate for me to ask you what you do for a living?" Soon I had the bank employees stopping by for lobster rolls, and the Ninety-fifth Precinct and a list of celebrities (to this day, I've kept my promise that I wouldn't reveal their names). People loved the adventure. Even better, I was making real money for the first time in my life.

One day I received an official notice: "To Benjamin F. W. Sargent, DBA the Lobstah Pusherman/Dr. Klaw. By order of the Commissioner of the Board of Health: Cease and desist!" "You will be sent to prison." I had it framed, and it hangs in my apartment.

Dr. Klaw was forced into retirement, but I gained notoriety and hosted my own Cooking Channel show, *Hook, Line & Dinner*. Long live Dr. Klaw!

You don't need to be a fisherman to make these recipes. Just buy the highest-quality, freshest fish you can and follow the instructions.

MY KIND OF COOKBOOK

I am a cook. I find the word *chef* too high-toned for my approach to food. I enrolled in culinary school, but after one day in chef whites, I knew I wasn't cut out for that super-regimented world. That didn't stop me from cooking, though, and this book is the result of years of traveling the world, catching fish, and cooking them. I think it is important that people eat what they catch and catch what they eat. It gives them a deeper appreciation of the value of the bounty of the oceans, rivers, lakes, and streams. I believe in taking just enough to feed yourself. If I want to fish for fun, I release the fish I don't plan to eat. You don't need to be a fisherman to make these recipes, though. Just buy the highest-quality, freshest fish you can and follow the instructions.

Probably more than half of my diet is made up of fish I have caught. Okay, I get to fish more than most people. But my point is that when you fish to eat, you end up appreciating all fish, and all life, even more. If you love to fish, you can't help but become a bit of a conservationist and that's a very good thing.

Fishing brings with it a HUGE responsibility to respect the resources so our wild fisheries are here for generations to come. This is a tall order in a world of exploding population and ever more effective—and lethal—fish-catching technology. I have my strong opinions about what fish to lay off of for now—the magnificent and endangered bluefin tuna, for example. And I would urge you to check these few websites if you ever have a question about how sustainable a fishery is. Here are my three favorites:

1. Seafood Watch from the Monterey Bay Aquarium in Monterey, California
   www.montereybayaquarium.org/cr/-seafoodwatch.aspx

2. The Blue Ocean Institute
   www.blueocean.org/programs/sustainable-seafood-program/

3. The Marine Stewardship Council
   www.msc.org/cook-eat-enjoy/fish-to-eat

Every recipe in here is going to be super-fun and not super-difficult. If it isn't fun and easy, it's not a Dr. Klaw kind of dish! True, some recipes take more time or require more ingredients, but if you can chop and heat, those are about all the cooking techniques you need to cook your way through this book.

SHELLFISH

& more

CLAMS

I was born and bred on the hard-shell New England clams we call quahogs. Now, when you say quahog to a New Englander you are usually talking about the large members of this species prized for chowder and stews. Non–New Englanders are sometimes shocked by quahogs because of their sheer size and meatiness (they're pretty briny, like a North Atlantic oyster). One big quahog can make a meal; once you find a monster and chop it up, it'll be enough meat for an entire chowder. Technically speaking, littlenecks and cherrystones are the same animal, just smaller, and better suited to roasting and stuffing or eating on the half shell.

We had quahogs—big and small—in front of our house in Orleans on Cape Cod, where my dad had an uncanny ability to find them in shallow waters. He would just feel for them by wiggling his toes, and when he felt one, he'd reach down and come up with a clam in his hand. Amazing! I still can't do it like he did, though believe me, I have spent years trying.

Also very popular in New England are soft-shell or steamer clams. They have a different texture and are very sweet, with a long neck. Many people like them simply steamed and served with a little butter, and just as many folks like to add them for some variety in their chowder.

Last, but by no means least, is the wonderful razor clam. Razor clams are really sweet, too. If you could take the tastiest, meatiest part of the quahog and make it bigger and sweeter, that's what a razor clam is like for me. Some people shy away from them because they haven't heard of 'em before—and, to be fair, razor clams don't really resemble a clam shape. They're not rounded. Instead they are long and thin and look . . . well . . . just like an old-fashioned straight

razor. If you're new to seafood or want to introduce someone to clams, razor clams are great starter clams because they don't have the big belly and sandy, gritty guts of quahogs.

My love affair with the razor clam goes back to my early fishing days. Neither my dad nor my grandfather thought a boat weighted down with fish qualified as a one-hundred-percent successful day on the water, so after hauling whatever we caught out of the boat and rowing the dingy to shore, we would hit the family clam flats. Razor clams were so fun to dig for, because *they* dig even faster than you can, so it's like a race between man and clam. The idea of ambushing a clam might sound odd, but this is exactly what you have to do with them. Don't step on or near their hole; just sneak up and start digging from a side angle. If you get under them before they can start their getaway, you might have a chance.

Preparation warning: Razor clams live up to their name. Be careful when you open them; I know from experience that they cut like their barbershop namesake.

One big quahog can make a meal;
once you find a monster and chop
it up, it'll be enough meat for an
entire chowder.

SARGE'S CLAM CHOWDER

This is a basic rustic chowder you are going to fall in love with. I used to marvel at my grandfather's enthusiasm for making chowder because even after a full day of fishing he always wanted to dig for clams—lots of 'em and all kinds. Because of the variety of clams on the tidal flats in front of our house on Cape Cod, the recipe always came out a little different each time. That was part of the fun of it. You can make this only using quahogs, but usually, when we did the gathering, some steamers and razors found their way in, too.

I made this on the *Martha Stewart Show*. Martha asked me if it really needed heavy cream. If you want to make it the way Pup did, that's the way you do it. To me, changing his recipe would be like changing the words to the *Star-Spangled Banner.* Some things are sacred, even if they are fattening.

20 pounds quahog clams, or a combination of quahogs, steamers, and razor clams

¼ cup dry white wine

2 bay leaves

½ teaspoon black peppercorns

¼ pound salt pork, skin removed, cut into ¼-inch dice

¼ pound bacon, cut into 1-inch dice

2 tablespoons olive oil

3 pounds medium Yukon Gold potatoes, partially peeled and quartered

2 large sweet onions, cut into 1-inch dice

12 plum tomatoes, chopped

1 small fennel bulb, trimmed and thinly sliced

1 garlic clove, minced

4 tablespoons (½ stick) unsalted butter, plus more for serving

1 teaspoon fresh thyme leaves

6 cups heavy cream

2 tablespoons chopped fresh dill

1 tablespoon steak sauce

¼ teaspoon Old Bay seasoning

5 drops Worcestershire sauce

5 capers

Salt and freshly ground black pepper

Herb sprigs such as tarragon or sage, for garnish

SERVES 8 TO 10

1 Scrub the clams and rinse well. Keep the kinds of clams in their own groups. Put a very large steamer pot on the stove and add 6 cups of water, the wine, bay leaves, and peppercorns and bring to a boil. First, layer in the quahogs, then arrange the steamers over that. Top with the razor clams, but if there is no room, cook them in the next batch. Cover and cook over high heat until boiling and the clams open, about 15 minutes. With tongs, transfer them as they open to a couple of large bowls. When all the clams are cooked, let cool slightly, and while working over another medium bowl, pull the meat from all the shells, leave the two tough pink muscles on each side of the shell, and drop in the bowl, saving all of the juices. Set a strainer over a large bowl and strain the clam juices from the pot. Pour slowly, stopping when you reach grit at the bottom. Measure out 6 cups of the clam juice and freeze the rest for another use.

2 Meanwhile, in a large heavy pot, cook the salt pork over medium-high heat, stirring, until crisp, about 5 minutes. With a slotted spoon, transfer the salt pork to paper towels to drain and pour the fat into a separate small bowl. Add the bacon and cook over medium heat until cooked through but not too crisp, about 5 minutes. Transfer the bacon to paper towels to drain, leaving ¼ cup of the fat in the pot. Add the olive oil and potatoes and cook over medium heat, stirring a few times, until the potatoes begin to soften and are golden, about 20 minutes. Add the onions, tomatoes, fennel, and garlic along with the butter and thyme and cook, stirring a few times, until softened, about 10 minutes.

3 Meanwhile, pull the skin from the long necks of the steamer and razor clams and discard. Cut the clams into strips and leave the bellies whole. Cut the solid parts from around the quahogs into ½-inch pieces and leave the bellies whole. You can reserve a few whole steamers and razors for garnishing the chowder.

4 Add the 6 cups of clam juice to the pot and stir well to blend with the potatoes and onions. Stir in the reserved fat from the salt pork, the heavy cream, dill, and the clam meat and simmer for 10 minutes. Use a wooden spoon or fork and periodically, as the potatoes soften, crush them against the side of the pot, to thicken the soup. Add the bacon and cook for 20 minutes. Then add the steak sauce, Old Bay, Worcestershire sauce, and capers, and simmer gently for about 35 minutes.

5 Discard the bay leaves. Season the chowder with salt and pepper if necessary, and ladle into bowls. Serve with a pat of butter and the salt pork cracklings. Garnish with herb sprigs and serve.

The chowder can be refrigerated for up to 3 days.

Rockaway Beach STUFFIES

This is one of my signature recipes. The stuffies are brimming with flavor and are packed so full that they look like little golden balls of goodness! They're fun and you can get your guests involved in making them. Even for non-cooks, it's hard to mess this one up. When they are all cooked and ready to serve, they look like irresistible cookies on a plate. I use every last bit of the clam—shell, meat, and juice—to really pump up the clam flavor. People ask me why they're called stuffies. Because I'm from Massachusetts, and when we stuff a clam shell it isn't a stretch to call the finished product a stuffy. I have made this with my surf buddies in the Rockaways using Long Island clams.

16 large clam shells, about 4 inches across

5 tablespoons olive oil, plus more for the shells

4 hot Italian sausages (about 12 ounces), casings removed

2 medium onions, finely diced

8 (5-ounce) cans chopped clams, drained, 1 cup of juices reserved

2 (10-ounce) cans whole baby clams, drained

2 cups Italian bread crumbs

2 garlic cloves, minced

1 tablespoon Old Bay seasoning, plus more for dusting

1 cup chopped fresh cilantro

Freshly ground black pepper

1 cup grated Parmesan

8 scallions, white and green parts, thinly sliced

Makes 16 clams;
SERVES 6 TO 8

1 Clean the shells under hot water and dry with paper towels. Lightly oil the insides of the shells.

2 In a large skillet, heat 1 tablespoon of the olive oil and add the sausage. Cook over medium-high heat, breaking it up, for about 3 minutes. Reduce the heat to medium and cook, continuing to break up the sausage, until no pink remains, about 4 minutes longer. Transfer the sausage to a large bowl. Add 2 tablespoons of the olive oil to the skillet and add the onions. Cook over medium heat, stirring often, until slightly softened, about 6 minutes. Add the onions to the bowl with the sausage.

3 Add the remaining 2 tablespoons of olive oil, the chopped and whole drained clams, the reserved clam juice, bread crumbs, garlic, Old Bay, and cilantro. Season with black pepper. With a wooden spoon, mix the stuffing well until very tight. Pack the stuffing neatly into the clam shells.

4 Preheat the broiler. Set the oven rack 10 inches from the broiler heat source. Put half the clams on a cookie sheet and dust thickly with half the Parmesan. Sprinkle with some Old Bay and scatter half the scallions on top. Broil the clams until hot throughout and nicely glazed, about 10 minutes. Repeat with the remaining clams. Let rest for about 5 minutes and serve.

The stuffies can be frozen for up to 1 month. Thaw, dust with the Parmesan and Old Bay, and top with the scallions before broiling.

People ask me why they're called stuffies. Because I'm from Massachusetts, and when we stuff a clam shell, it isn't a stretch to call the finished product a stuffy.

Stacked & Spicy RAZOR CLAMS
WITH ANGEL HAIR PASTA

This is a very simple recipe, and it is really delicious. The fun part for me is the presentation. If you have ever started a campfire by laying down a couple of twigs and then laying another pair of twigs crosswise and repeating until you have built a little "log cabin," then you have this presentation down. Or maybe you did the same thing with pickup sticks. Either way, place a ball of already sauced pasta in the middle of your plate and arrange the clams into a little cabin around the pasta, which look like rolled bales of hay.

Vegetable oil, for frying

1 fresh long red chile, thinly sliced

4 small shallots, thinly sliced, separated into rings

4 tablespoons (½ stick) unsalted butter

4 garlic cloves, minced

1 jalapeño, seeded and thinly sliced

¼ cup soy sauce

½ cup white wine

Salt

½ pound angel hair pasta

3 pounds razor clams

Freshly ground black pepper

¼ cup chopped fresh cilantro or flat-leaf parsley

SERVES 4

1 In a large, deep skillet, heat ⅛ inch of oil. Add the red chile slices and cook over medium-high heat until starting to brown, about 2 minutes. With a slotted spoon, transfer the chiles to a plate. Add the shallot rings to the hot oil and cook over medium-low heat, stirring a few times to keep the rings separated, until browned and crisp, about 4 minutes. With the slotted spoon, transfer the shallots to the plate.

2 Pour off all but 1 tablespoon of the oil and add the butter to melt. Add the garlic and jalapeño and cook over medium heat until fragrant, about 2 minutes. Add the soy sauce and simmer for about 1 minute to reduce slightly. Add the wine and ¼ cup of water, cover, and turn off the heat.

3 Bring a large pot of salted water to a boil and add the pasta. Cook, stirring, until al dente, about 3 minutes.

4 Meanwhile, bring the garlic-jalapeño mixture to a boil over medium-high heat. Have a large bowl near the stove. Add the clams to the skillet, cover, and cook, shaking the skillet a few times, until the clams open, 3 to 4 minutes. With the slotted spoon, transfer the clams to the bowl and cover. Discard any clams that do not open.

5 Drain the pasta and add to the skillet. Cook over medium-low heat, stirring, until the pasta has absorbed most of the sauce, about 1 minute. Season with salt and pepper. Divide the pasta and sauce among 4 shallow bowls. Stack the clams around the pasta while scattering the fried red chiles and shallots all over. Sprinkle with the cilantro and serve.

MANILA CLAMS
WITH FRIED GARLIC, HABANERO & GINGER

Originally from Asia, Manila clams are now mostly farmed in the United States, although I have also dug for them in the wild. They have gained popularity because they are so small, sweet, and tender. They remind me of the juicy, sweet vongole I have had in Venice with some pasta, oil, and garlic. In a nod to its Asian roots, I make this recipe with steamed rice and accent it with a simple combination of ginger, chile, and soy sauce. I once found a real expert a few hours outside of San Francisco to teach me an Italian pasta dish. Well, turns out this guy had been sent to prison for poaching fish illegally for years and was fresh out of the slammer. I was not happy to find this out but I was glad to learn so much from him about Manila clams!

3 tablespoons vegetable oil

¼ cup peeled fresh ginger, cut into small thin sticks

8 garlic cloves, thinly sliced

1 habanero chile, thinly sliced

Salt

¼ cup soy sauce

3 pounds Manila clams, scrubbed

2 tablespoons unsalted butter

½ cup thinly sliced fresh basil

3 to 4 cups steamed sushi rice

SERVES 4

1 In a large pot or Dutch oven, warm the oil. Add the ginger sticks in an even layer and cook over medium heat until they start to brown, about 2 minutes. Add the garlic and when it starts to sizzle, spread out the slices evenly. Cook, undisturbed, over medium-low heat for 1 minute. Scatter the habanero slices over, sprinkle with a little salt, and continue to cook until the garlic is golden, about 3 minutes longer. Tilt the pot and, with a slotted spoon, transfer the chile mixture to a small bowl.

2 Add the soy sauce to the oil in the pot and boil over medium-high heat until slightly reduced, about 1 minute. Add the clams, cover, and cook, shaking the pot a few times, until they open, about 4 minutes. Discard any clams that do not open.

3 Set a medium skillet on the stove. With the lid over the clams slightly ajar, pour the clam liquid into the skillet. Boil the liquid over high heat until reduced to about ¾ cup and very flavorful, about 1 minute. Remove the skillet from the heat and stir in the butter, 1 tablespoon at a time. Stir in the reserved chile mixture.

4 Divide the clams among 4 shallow bowls. Pour the sauce over, top each with some basil, and serve right away. Pass the steamed rice at the table.

CONCH

The conch—a giant sea snail—is a tradiional food of poor folks in the Caribbean, no doubt because it was plentiful, although like all wild fisheries, overfishing has depleted its numbers. I owe my introduction to the conch to Meagan Soloff, a school friend from Boston. Growing up, we would often skip class to hit our favorite Chinese restaurant around the corner from school. Meagan used to tell me, "When I grow up, I'm going to open a Chinese restaurant." This, from a nice Jewish girl from Boston.

As school friends often do, we lost touch. Years later, I was on a family trip to St. John in the Virgin Islands. I had split off on my own to recon the island and found myself on the second floor of a mini mall where sailors would come for groceries. At the end of the hallway, I saw a sign: MEAGAN'S CHINA SHACK.

"No way . . . ," I said to myself.

I went inside and asked, "Does a Meagan Soloff by any chance run this place?"

"Yeah, she does . . . would you like to say hi?"

"No way, it couldn't be her," I thought. But it was the very same Meagan. At the end of our family vacation I announced at the airport that I was staying on to work with Meagan. I figured I had a surfboard and a job delivering Chinese food and I was in Paradise. What more did I really need? Now if she would just let me near the wok.

I spent the next few months delivering Meagan's Chinese food with a Rasta by the name of Gangster. We must have been quite a sight: one big guy with dreadlocks who looked like Bob Marley's bodyguard and the other, a white surfer dude, delivering Chinese food!

I served this chowder at my first
restaurant, Hurricane Hopeful.
Die-hard customers liked it so much
that some often came for it twice a
day. It's also the chowder I made
on the very first *Throwdown with
Bobby Flay*. It came out great,
but Bobby won.

CURRIED BAHAMAS CONCH CHOWDER

The first conch chowder I ever had was after a long day of trying to find my aunt Jay's dolphin friend, named JoJo, who swims in the waters off the Turks and Caicos islands. Jay has had close encounters with JoJo for years, but after I spent three days chasing him without a sighting I was beginning to think JoJo might have been her imaginary friend. But lo and behold, he finally showed up like a family dog who'd been off chasing a deer in the woods. Just as my aunt had promised, he frolicked with her for an hour. They were so happy to see each other! And sure enough, just as Jay told me, when I jumped in, JoJo was gone! Just like that, in an instant: gone! When I swam up on some conch under a big pirate wreck I was delighted and grabbed a bunch. We ate half as a ceviche and we took the rest to the home of my aunt's friend George, who made a wonderful conch chowder!

2 tablespoons unsalted butter

1½ pounds fresh or frozen cleaned conch, thawed, cut into ½-inch-wide strips

1 large Spanish onion, halved, thinly sliced

Salt and freshly ground black pepper

2 red bell peppers, cored, seeded, and cut into ½-inch dice

2 green bell peppers, cored, seeded, and cut into ½-inch dice

3 tablespoons Jamaican curry powder

½ teaspoon cayenne pepper

½ teaspoon sweet paprika

1 bay leaf

1 quart heavy cream

3 cups Fish Stock (page 113), clam juice, or vegetable stock

1 (28-ounce) can whole tomatoes, crushed by hand, with juices

2 (13-ounce) cans unsweetened coconut milk

¼ cup cream of coconut, such as Coco López

3 pounds Idaho potatoes, peeled and cut into 1-inch dice

2 large carrots, cut into ½-inch dice

2 large green plantains, peeled and cut into 1-inch dice

2 large yellow plantains, peeled and cut into 1-inch dice

1 pound firm white fish fillet, such as mahimahi, skinned, cut into ½-inch pieces

¼ cup chopped fresh flat-leaf parsley

Hot sauce, for serving

SERVES 8 TO 10

1. In a large pot, melt the butter. Add the conch and onion, season with salt and pepper, and cook over medium heat, stirring, until the onion is translucent, about 10 minutes. Add the red and green bell peppers and cook until soft, about 8 minutes. Add the curry powder, cayenne, paprika, bay leaf, and a pinch of salt. Cook, stirring, until fragrant, about 3 minutes.

2. Add the cream, stock, tomatoes with juices, coconut milk, and cream of coconut and stir well. Add the potatoes, carrots, and the green and yellow plantains and bring to a brisk simmer. Cook over low heat, stirring occasionally, until the conch and plantains are tender, about 1½ hours.

3. Add the fish and simmer for a few minutes, until the fish is just cooked and starts to flake. Discard the bay leaf, add the parsley, and season with salt and pepper. Serve with hot sauce at the table.

Martha's Vineyard CONCH PANCAKES

This is a different kind of seafood fritter, a crisp flat pancake that reminds me of the oyster pancakes I find in Korean restaurants. It's filled with conch pieces and served with a spicy dipping sauce. The thing I particularly like about this recipe is that it is kind of light and our northern conch works well in it. I first attempted these fritters in Menemsha on Martha's Vineyard. I was doing a demo for a bunch of fishermen and tourists when I had this idea for a conch pancake. It was a complete disaster. I had way too much batter in my first version. People began to go home as it became apparent my pancake was never going to cook. Eventually, I perfected the recipe. You can use fresh or frozen conch for all conch dishes, but be sure to pound the conch with a meat pounder in order to tenderize it if you are going to use big chunks. For this one, I prefer to slice it thin so that no tenderizing is needed.

1 cup all-purpose flour

½ cup cornstarch

½ teaspoon salt

1 large egg

¼ cup vegetable oil

4 scallions, halved crosswise, very thinly sliced

1 red bell pepper, cored, seeded, and thinly sliced

1 jalapeño, seeded and thinly sliced

1 pound cleaned conch, fresh or frozen, pounded and cut into ¼-inch to ½-inch dice

Lemon wedges

Asian hot sauce

Soy sauce

SERVES 4

1 In a large bowl, whisk together the flour, cornstarch, and salt. In a medium bowl, whisk the egg with 1¾ cups of water. Whisk the egg mixture into the flour mixture.

2 Heat an 8-inch nonstick skillet. Add 1 tablespoon of the oil, and when hot, add one quarter of the scallions, bell pepper, and jalapeño. Cook over high heat until starting to wilt, about 1 minute. Add one quarter of the conch and spread it out evenly. Add ⅓ cup of the batter and tilt the pan to evenly distribute. Cook over high heat until browned and crisp on the bottom, about 3 minutes. Flip the cake and cook about 30 seconds longer. Slide the cake onto a plate and serve, passing lemon, hot sauce, and soy sauce for topping. Repeat with the remaining ingredients to make 3 more cakes.

Most of the time, conch fritters are like hush puppies: big, round, and heavy (though delicious). Mine are flatter with more overall crispiness.

CRABS

It's fair to say I respect all crabs. Why? I have battle scars to prove what they did to me as a kid. I can also say that I am somewhat of a master crabber after all these years. I can catch 'em with my bare hands, net 'em, and spear 'em. Spearing is practical; it's where you don't puncture the shell, you just pin them down. Once you have them pinned, you go around the back side of them and pinch the swim flippers. The crab can't get you if you do it right. But I like to net them. Some people remove the crabs each time they pull up the net, but I find that once they cling to the net they tend to stay there. So rather than stopping to put them in a bucket and then netting again, I just keep on plunging the net. You might lose a few crabs in the process, but most will stay clinging to the net.

One day, when I was five years old, I went crabbing in Chilmark Pond on Martha's Vineyard. I was overjoyed to be with my crabbing idol, a nine-year-old kid named Josh. We both had our nets, and when I walked over to his pail, I told him he shouldn't be taking the females (little environmentalist smartass that I was) because it was bad for reproduction. A look of awe and appreciation flashed on his face. I taught Josh how to flip the crabs over and identify them. The next day he went to Alley's general store and spent all of his allowance on a gift for me—a gorgeous plastic dump truck, which effectively made Josh my idol, hero, and friend.

Blue crabbing has always been my thing. Every year we'd do what we called The Cut, and take a bulldozer down to Chilmark Pond to open it to the sea. This produced pure mayhem as fish poured out of the pond into the ocean. I would paddle out on my surfboard and marvel at the standing wave that rushed out of the pond. I'd look down into the water while riding my board and watch bluefish and stripers massacre a torrent of fresh baitfish. Once the water leveled out, baitfish such as bunker (menhaden) and blue crabs would make their way into the pond. The next year's crabbing was pretty much determined on that one day.

CRAB & CORN CHOWDER
WITH FLAMBÉED CRABS

This chowder is a bit of a project, but it feeds a large group and it's spectacular. The fireworks come with flambéing the crabs at the end. It took me a long time to get this chowder recipe right, but once I did, I knew I had a crowd-pleaser. I once made it on the docks on the Vineyard and I am proud to report that Buddy Vanderhoop, a Wampanoag Native American and an eighth-generation Martha's Vineyard commercial fisherman, said it's the best chowder he ever had.

Chowder

3 tablespoons olive oil

8 medium red potatoes, quartered

4 tablespoons (½ stick) unsalted butter

2 medium onions, cut into medium dice

2 leeks, white and light green parts, sliced crosswise 1 inch wide, rinsed well and patted dry

2 garlic cloves, minced

2 teaspoons chopped fresh thyme

1 teaspoon chopped fresh rosemary

½ teaspoon Old Bay seasoning

Salt and freshly ground black pepper

1 quart Seafood Stock (opposite)

2 quarts whole milk

2 cups Creamed Corn (page 242)

1½ pounds striped bass fillets, skinned and cut into 1-inch cubes

1½ pounds lump blue-claw crab meat, picked over for shell

Shelled shrimp, reserved from Seafood Stock

½ cup chopped fresh cilantro

Flambéed crabs

5 cooked crabs, from Seafood Stock

1 tablespoon olive oil

1 small red onion, minced

1 garlic clove, minced

1 tablespoon tomato paste

Salt

2 tablespoons cognac or brandy

SERVES 10

1 To make the chowder: In a large pot, heat the olive oil and add the potatoes. Cook over medium heat, stirring a few times, until softened and golden, about 10 minutes. Add the butter along with the onions, leeks, garlic, thyme, rosemary, and Old Bay, and season with salt and pepper. Stir well and cook until the onions and leeks are soft, about 10 minutes. Add the stock and simmer over medium-high heat for 15 minutes. Add the milk and creamed corn and bring to a simmer. Cook over low heat, stirring and mashing some of the potatoes with a fork against the side of the pot once they get soft, about 30 minutes.

2 Add the bass pieces to the chowder and simmer until almost cooked and starting to flake, about 3 minutes. Add the crab meat and shrimp and stir in gently. Simmer 1 or 2 minutes, until the fish and shrimp are just cooked, then season with salt and pepper.

3 Prepare the flambéed crabs: Gently lift the top shells off the crabs without pulling the tops off, and pull out the spongy lungs on each side. Put the shell back and with a large knife, cut the crabs in half. In a large, nonstick skillet, heat the olive oil. Add the onion and garlic and cook over medium heat until soft and starting to brown, about 8 minutes. Stir in the tomato paste until smooth. Add the halved crabs, top shells up, and cook until heated through, about 4 minutes. Season lightly with salt and remove from the heat. Raise the heat under the crabs to medium-high and cook until hot and sizzling. Add the cognac, carefully light with a long-handled match, and stand back. Shake the pan until the flames die down.

4 Ladle the chowder into bowls and place a crab half in each bowl along with some of the garlic-onion mixture in the skillet. Garnish with cilantro and serve.

The recipe can be prepared through Step 1 and refrigerated for up to 2 days.

SEAFOOD STOCK (CRAB STOCK)

1 pound shrimp, shelled and deveined, shells reserved

3½ to 4 pounds white fish head and skeleton, such as striped bass

5 bay leaves

2 carrots, sliced ½ inch thick

1 teaspoon black peppercorns

½ cup dry white wine

Salt

5 live crabs, and/or 1 pound shrimp in their shells, and/or 1 pound lobster pieces in their shells

MAKES ABOUT 3 QUARTS

To amp up the flavor in a stock, I will add a pound or so of crab, shrimp, or lobster to a basic fish stock recipe.

In a large pot, combine the shrimp shells, fish head and skeleton, bay leaves, carrots, peppercorns, wine, 3 quarts of water, and a pinch of salt. Cover and bring to a boil over high heat, about 15 minutes, to cook the fish bones. Discard the fish head and skeleton and add the crabs. Simmer over medium heat until the crabs are red all over, 3 to 4 minutes. With tongs, transfer the crabs to a large bowl and reserve. Simmer the stock for 1 hour. Strain and add a little salt.

The seafood stock can be refrigerated overnight or frozen for up to 1 month. Gently reheat and proceed.

Spicy SOFT-SHELL CRABS
WITH LEMON SHALLOT SAUCE

When crabs molt and start to grow a new shell that is soft in the beginning, they are a real treat. You can eat the whole crab! The best way to cook soft-shell crabs is by frying in hot oil. The crabs crisp up quickly and they won't absorb too much oil. I like to arrange the crabs in a circle around some lemon wedges with their little claws sticking out at you. Something about the panko and the way it crisps up on the crabs makes 'em look so yummy!

2 medium shallots, minced

5 tablespoons unsalted butter, cut into tablespoons, chilled

1 garlic clove, minced

⅔ cup white wine

½ cup Fish Stock (page 113) or ¼ cup clam juice with ¼ cup water

2 teaspoons finely grated lemon zest

Vegetable oil, for frying

All-purpose flour, for dredging

2 large eggs, beaten

2 cups panko bread crumbs

2 teaspoons salt

1 teaspoon freshly ground black pepper

1 teaspoon cayenne pepper

6 large soft-shelled crabs, eyes and aprons (the abdominal shell) cut off, lungs cut out

3 scallions, chopped

SERVES 4 TO 6

1 In a medium saucepan, cook the shallots in 1 tablespoon butter on low heat for 4 minutes until softened but not browned. Add the garlic and cook for 1 minute. Add the wine and boil over high heat until reduced by half. Add the stock and boil until the liquid is reduced to ½ cup. Add half the zest, remove from the heat, and let cool a bit until just hot. Whisk in the remaining chilled butter, 1 tablespoon at a time, until the sauce is smooth. Put the saucepan back over medium heat, whisking, for about 10 seconds or so to keep the sauce very warm. Do not let the sauce get too hot or simmer, or it will separate. Put it off and on the burner as needed. Remove from the heat and let stand for up to 1 hour.

2 In a large, deep cast-iron frying pan or heavy pot, heat 1 inch of oil to 360°F. Set up 3 wide, shallow bowls or pie plates. Place flour in the first one, the beaten eggs and 3 tablespoons of water in the second, and the panko, salt, pepper, cayenne, and remaining 1 teaspoon of zest in the third. Stir the panko mixture to combine well.

3 Have a large rack set over a large rimmed baking sheet near the stove. Dredge 2 or 3 crabs at a time in the flour, shaking off excess, then in the egg mixture, and finally in the panko mixture. Carefully lay the crabs in the hot oil (they will splatter, so use a splatter screen). Cook for 1 to 2 minutes per side. Remove with tongs to the rack to drain. Repeat with the remaining crabs.

4 Reheat the lemon shallot sauce by stirring it constantly over medium heat; do not let it simmer or boil. Spoon the sauce over each crab and sprinkle with scallions. Serve immediately on warmed plates. Cut the crabs in half to serve 1½ crabs per person if desired.

This is great finger food, and it's easy enough to make. I have prepared this dish many times on the camp stove in the little trailer I used to pull with my old Land Cruiser.

If you have one of those wire mesh fish baskets used to grill fillets, you can put the stuffed poblanos right in there. Clamp it down and grill over the open fire to give them a little smoky flavor. Killer!

Open Fire CRAB-STUFFED ROASTED POBLANOS

I have made this dish so many times. I even replaced crab with alligator once. I first learned it from a chef and crab trapper in the Southeast who wants to remain anonymous. My friend knew I was crazy into surfing and he told me he had a secret surf spot offshore that he would take me to. However, just to make sure that I kept it secret I had to wear a bag over my head for the whole voyage! I confess that I was actually a little scared. But, as promised, we arrived to find good surf and then crab-a-palooza! We gathered crabs and created this dish on the spot.

6 poblano peppers

5 tablespoons unsalted butter

1 large shallot, minced

1 celery stalk, finely diced

¼ red bell pepper, cored, seeded, and finely diced

¼ yellow bell pepper, cored, seeded, and finely diced

1 teaspoon finely grated lemon zest

½ teaspoon sweet paprika

2 tablespoons mayonnaise

½ pound lump crab meat

Salt and freshly ground black pepper

1 teaspoon Old Bay seasoning

1 cup panko bread crumbs

SERVES 6

1 Over a gas flame, or under the broiler, roast the poblanos, turning frequently, until blackened and blistered all over. Place in a large bowl, cover with plastic wrap, and let stand for about 10 minutes. Remove the blackened skin from the peppers. Carefully make a slit in the front of the pepper and with scissors, snip out the seed head under the stem, then clean out all of the seeds.

2 In a large skillet, melt 1 tablespoon of the butter. Add the shallot, celery, and red and yellow bell peppers and cook the vegetables over low heat for about 4 minutes, until softened but not colored. Scrape into a large bowl and cool.

3 Add the zest, paprika, and mayonnaise to the vegetables. Gently fold in the crab meat and season with salt and pepper. Stuff each pepper with the crab mixture, closing the pepper around the mixture.

4 Preheat the oven to 350°F. In a small saucepan, melt the remaining 4 tablespoons of butter, then stir in the Old Bay and panko and blend well.

5 Put the stuffed poblanos on an oiled rimmed baking sheet and bake for about 7 minutes, until heated through. Remove from the oven, turn on the broiler, and top the stuffed poblanos with the panko mixture. Broil about 6 inches from the heat for about 2 minutes or until the panko is crisp. Place a pepper on each plate and serve.

The roasted, unfilled poblanos and crab filling can be refrigerated overnight. Take the chill off before filling.

CRAYFISH

Crayfish, crawfish, crawdads, or mudbugs, as they are affectionately and interchangeably known, are much loved in the South, which is the only place they are commercially raised. Think of them as bite-size, soft, sweet mini lobsters. I have speared them, charged after 'em by hand in little rivers and brooks. I have pulled them out of traps and used a baited bucket and a tin can. I like catching crawfish because you can run 'em down in a creek by yourself and if they pinch you, it's gentle compared to, say, the blue crab! I've seen and used a number of different cool handmade apparatuses to catch them, and almost all of them have worked because no one ever used the words *crawdads* and *cunning* in the same sentence.

I've also gone up against the fastest crawdad eater in the United States. Sweltering in the Louisiana heat in 2010, he would rip off the head and squeeze the tail and shoot the meat into his mouth, one crawfish after another. He ate four or five in the time it took me to eat one. I was so desperate not to be destroyed in the competition that I grabbed the whole thing and shoved it into my mouth, shell and all. It was cheating, but I was just getting beat too bad. When the competition was over, with crawfish all over me, I met beauty contest winner Ms. Crawfish, bedecked in a tiara. I did not notice a look of admiration coming over her face as she glanced at the mess I had made of myself.

CRAYFISH RISOTTO
WITH CELERY ROOT & WATERCRESS

Instead of trapping your own crayfish, you can take the easy way out, which is fine (I have done the same) and just buy crayfish tails, cooked and shelled. Even though they come with their own beautiful orange fat, more butter is needed to draw out all the crayfish flavor and richness. Their soft, meaty texture makes for a more delicate risotto than shrimp does. Use a crayfish stock if you have it (or Fish Stock on page 113). Spanish Valencia or Bomba rice makes a very nice risotto; the grain is a bit smaller and pearl-like.

¾ pound celery root, peeled and cut into ½-inch dice

2½ tablespoons olive oil

Salt and freshly ground black pepper

3 tablespoons unsalted butter

1 garlic clove, minced

½ pound cooked, shelled crayfish tails with their fat

1 tablespoon fresh lemon juice

5 cups Fish Stock (page 113) or 2 cups clam juice and 3 cups water

½ small onion, minced

1 cup Arborio or Valencia rice

1 teaspoon finely grated lemon zest

1 tablespoon grated Parmesan

2 cups small watercress sprigs

SERVES 4

1 Preheat the oven to 375°F. Place the celery root pieces on a rimmed baking sheet and drizzle with 1 tablespoon of the olive oil. Toss the celery root to coat with the oil and arrange in an even layer. Season with salt and pepper and bake for about 20 minutes, until browned and tender.

2 Meanwhile, in a small skillet, melt 2 tablespoons of the butter. Add the garlic and cook over low heat until fragrant, about 1 minute. Add the crayfish tails and all the fat surrounding them and cook, stirring, until hot. Remove the skillet from the heat and stir in the lemon juice.

3 In a medium saucepan, bring the stock to a boil. Cover and keep hot over very low heat. In a medium saucepan, heat 1 tablespoon of the olive oil. Add the onion and cook over medium heat until softened, about 4 minutes. Add the rice and cook, stirring, for 1 minute. Add enough hot stock to just cover the rice and cook, stirring, until the stock has been absorbed. Continue to cook and add stock, stirring constantly, until the rice is tender but a bit firm and is bound in a tight sauce, about 25 minutes total cooking time. Stir in the remaining 1 tablespoon of butter, the lemon zest, and Parmesan and season with salt and pepper.

4 Gently reheat the crayfish mixture. In a medium bowl, toss the watercress with the remaining ½ tablespoon of olive oil and a pinch of salt. Fold the roasted celery root into the risotto and divide among 4 shallow bowls. Spoon the crayfish mixture over the risotto, top with the watercress, and serve right away.

Louisiana CRAWFISH ÉTOUFFÉE

If you had to pick one recipe that captures the essence of crawfish it is a Louisiana étouffée. A rich stew, it's one of the few dishes I thicken with flour, because nothing compares to a carefully and lovingly made nut-brown roux, and you need flour to make a roux. I make my étouffée with celery. This is a bone of contention among Cajun cooks, who often tell you that celery is used by Creoles but not Cajuns.

8 tablespoons (1 stick) unsalted butter

½ cup all-purpose flour

2 celery stalks, finely diced

1 small onion, finely diced

1 small green bell pepper, cored, seeded, and finely diced

6 garlic cloves, minced

1 cup Fish Stock (page 113) or clam juice

½ cup chopped fresh flat-leaf parsley

4 dashes Tabasco, or more to taste

½ teaspoon cayenne pepper

Salt and freshly ground black pepper

1 pound cooked, shelled crawfish tails with their fat

4 scallions, chopped

SERVES 6

1 In a large saucepan, melt the butter, then add the flour and cook over medium-low heat, whisking often, until richly browned. Add the celery, onion, and bell pepper and cook on low until the vegetables are softened, about 7 minutes. Add the garlic and cook another 3 minutes. Stir in the stock, 1 cup water, parsley, Tabasco, cayenne, and a pinch of salt and black pepper.

2 Add the crawfish tails, cover, and simmer on low for 20 minutes, stirring occasionally. Season with salt and black pepper and more Tabasco, if desired, then serve over rice, with scallions on top.

The étouffée can be refrigerated overnight.

A ROUX TIP:

"Hey boy . . . don't go by YOUR skin color to test that your roux looks right," the famous African American chef Mrs. Leah Chase told me. She was making the roux for a gumbo for me in her historic restaurant in New Orleans. "You way too much of a white boy. Your roux down here in Louisiana needs to look more the color of MY skin." Point taken. "Sorry, Leah. I get it now," I said.

I've also gone up against the fastest
crawdad eater in the United States.
Sweltering in the Louisiana heat in
2010, he would rip off the head and
squeeze the tail and shoot the meat
into his mouth, one crawfish after
another.

CRAWFISH GRITS
WITH BACON-TOMATO RAGOUT

Many folks outside of the South are unfamiliar with grits. But if you have had polenta, then you have had the Italian translation of grits. I have eaten shrimp and grits all over the South. Usually grits are thickened with cheese, but I decided to leave that out. The result is lighter with more of the subtle taste of the delicate, tender meat of the crawfish. Of course, the crawfish, tomato, and bacon in this are a wonderful trinity of flavor. Real stone-ground grits require a long cooking time, but I think they are worth it for flavor and texture. If you are in a rush, though, you can substitute quick-cooking grits.

Grits

1 cup whole milk

1 cup stone-ground grits

1 tablespoon unsalted butter

Salt and freshly ground black pepper

Crawfish

4 thick slices bacon, cut crosswise into thin sticks

3 tablespoons unsalted butter

8 scallions, cut into 1-inch lengths

4 garlic cloves, minced

⅛ teaspoon cayenne pepper

2 plum tomatoes, chopped

2 teaspoons capers, drained and chopped

1 tablespoon Worcestershire sauce

½ pound cooked, shelled crawfish tails with their fat

Salt and freshly ground black pepper

SERVES 4

1   To prepare the grits: In a medium saucepan, combine 3 cups of water and the milk and bring to a simmer. Slowly whisk in the grits and bring back to a simmer, whisking constantly. Cook over low heat, whisking often, until the grits are tender and thick, about 1 hour.

2   Meanwhile, to prepare the crawfish: In a large skillet, cook the bacon over medium heat until crisp, about 6 minutes. With a slotted spoon, transfer the bacon to paper towels to drain. Pour off all but 1 tablespoon of the bacon fat and add 1 tablespoon of the butter. Add the scallions, garlic, and cayenne and cook over medium-low heat until softened, about 6 minutes. Add the tomatoes and cook over medium heat until the tomatoes thicken, about 4 minutes. Add the capers and Worcestershire sauce and simmer for 1 minute. Add the cooked crawfish tails and cook for a few minutes to heat through. Stir in the remaining 2 tablespoons of butter, 1 tablespoon at a time. Remove from the heat and stir in the bacon. Season with salt and pepper.

3   When the grits are tender, stir in the 1 tablespoon butter and season with salt and pepper. Divide the grits among 4 shallow bowls. Spoon the crawfish, bacon, and tomato ragout over the grits and serve.

LOBSTAH

I have gone after lobsters in just about every way possible! I've used a tickle stick, which is a long stick with a hook on it that you use to prod the lobster. When the lobster feels the stick it naturally backs up into your hook. Pretty neat. I've also barehanded them, which takes a little bit of courage (or a lot of foolishness). I've gone after them with free dive gear, and with conventional old-fashioned lobster traps. Chances are if you have had a lobster that's how it was caught. Perhaps the weirdest way I've caught them is with a Hawaiian sling, which is basically a spear attached to a strong elastic band. I find lobsters fascinating. They are tender romantics when the male lobster protects the female while she molts and sheds her skin (and when that's done, she usually leaves and blows off her protector). They can be brutal cannibals, too. I guess lobsters are as contradictory and complex as the human beings who eat them.

Lobster first appeared on my plate when I was six years old. We were on the Vineyard. Tasting it was the first time I understood the phrase "died and gone to heaven." Actually, I'm not sure I knew that phrase when I was six, but it was definitely the feeling I got as I devoured these critters for the first time. According to family legend, I ate not one, but two entire two-and-a-quarter-pound lobsters that night, including the claws, tails, body, legs, and knuckles. My folks were delighted by this spectacle: Nothing made them happier than when I tried something new. I surely impressed everyone at the table.

Now that I am a grown-up, the lobsters I eat run a bit smaller than those Martha's Vineyard big boys. A pound and a half or a pound and a quarter has enough sweet succulent meat. Instead of one big lob, have two of these little guys and you'll be happy, but no less messy. That's part of the price of eating lobsters, but it's one I'm willing to pay.

KILLING LOBSTERS HUMANELY

There's no getting around the fact that you need to start with a live lobster. Otherwise it will lose flavor, taste, and texture. That means there is no getting around having to commit first-degree lobstercide in the kitchen. Some people are bothered by this, but I am not one of them. Face it, any meat that you eat—fish, fowl, or four-legged—was killed by somebody. With lobsters you have to do it yourself. My rule is that it is the most humane to do it quickly. I think steaming or splitting for grilling produce the best result with the least amount of unnecessary pain to the lobster.

Here's how I do it.

SPLIT LOBSTERS FOR GRILLING

Make a medium-high fire on an oiled grill. Hold the lobster on a cutting board with its belly down and, using a chef's knife, go in with a firm stroke from the back of the shell at the crease where the body meets the tail. At this point, the lobster is dead even though its nerves may fire and you'll notice some movement. It's very quick. Push down with the rest of the knife to split the lobster in two, running the knife right up into the head. Place on the grill immediately for about 12 minutes for smaller lobsters, and about 15 minutes for larger lobsters. Season with salt and pepper. The meat should be cooked but still moist.

STEAMED LOBSTERS

Fill a very large pot with water so it comes up the sides about 2 inches. Add 2 tablespoons of salt for each quart of water. Bring the water to a rolling boil, then put in the lobsters, head first, one at a time. (You can place the lobsters on a steaming rack or just add them directly to the pot.) Cover tightly, return to a boil as quickly as possible, and start counting the time according to the following chart.

Lobster Weight	Cooking Time
1¼ pounds	7–8 minutes
1½ pounds	8–10 minutes
2 pounds	11–12 minutes
2½ to 3 pounds	12–14 minutes
5 pounds	20–22 minutes

Lobsters are done when the outer shell is bright red and the meat is white, not opaque. A good test is to pull on an antenna and if it pulls out easily, your lobster is cooked. Carefully remove the lobsters from the pot with tongs; they will be very hot. Your lobsters will continue to cook after you take them out of the pot. To stop the cooking process, place your steamed lobsters in a bowl of ice before cracking.

GRILLED SPLIT LOBSTER

This is a very simple but always delicious recipe. If you have a large grill and are an especially diligent grill master, you can double the recipe and grill four whole lobsters if you wish. I've done as many as six at a time. If your lobsters have very large crusher claws (the claws with molar teeth) you may want to twist off the claws and grill them separately for more even cooking. It's important to keep the split lobsters level on the grill so the buttery juices remain in the head cavity as the lobsters cook and as you baste them with the juices.

2 (1½- to 1¾-pound) lobsters

2 garlic cloves, minced

6 tablespoons (¾ stick) unsalted butter

½ cup white wine

Salt and freshly ground black pepper

2 large limes, 1 juiced, 1 cut into wedges

2 tablespoons chopped fresh cilantro

SERVES 2

1 Light a grill. Put a lobster on a cutting board. Position a large, sharp knife point behind the eyes on top of the head. Cut down to cut the head in half. Turn the lobster the other way, flatten the tail, and cut through the rest of the body and the tail, cutting the lobster neatly in half. Discard the clear, sandy brain sac in the head and reserve the light green tamale. Discard the dark vein that runs down the tail. Press on the split tail to open it so it sits flat. With the heel of the knife, make cuts in the claws and knuckles. Twist off the claws if they are very large to grill separately. In each head, put one quarter of the garlic with ½ tablespoon of the butter.

2 Carefully put the lobsters on the grill cut sides up, set over a medium-low flame. Make sure the lobsters are level and try to keep in the juices that form in the head cavities. Arrange the claws, if possible, so they sit flat on the grill. Or set the separated claws flat on the grill. Add about 1 tablespoon of wine to each lobster head and season with salt and pepper. Let the lobsters grill slowly and build up juices in the head cavities. Add bits of butter and more wine as the lobsters cook, and baste the tail meat and cracks in the claws with the juices in the head. After about 15 minutes, add the tamale to the head cavities along with more butter, wine, and some of the lime juice. Keep basting the lobsters, moving them over hotter or cooler parts of the grill as needed, if possible without spilling the juices, to cook evenly. The separated claws can be turned occasionally, for even cooking. The lobsters should take about 30 minutes total cooking time. The tail meat should look almost all white and you should be able to pull off a little piece quite easily.

3 Just before removing the lobsters be sure there is plenty of juice and butter in the head cavities. Add more butter to melt, plus wine and lime juice as needed, then carefully transfer the lobsters to plates. Sprinkle with the cilantro and season again with salt and pepper. If the claws are still underdone, throw them back on the grill for a few minutes. Dip the claw meat in the juices, too. Serve with lime wedges.

LOBSTER BISQUE
WITH GINGERSNAP SWIMMERETS

Salt and freshly ground black pepper

3 (1¼-pound) lobsters

2 tablespoons olive oil

2 medium carrots, finely diced

1 medium onion, finely diced

6 thin slices peeled fresh ginger

2 large portobello mushrooms, stemmed, black gills cut off, caps cut into ½-inch dice

About 12 (2-inch) gingersnaps, crushed and ground in a food processor (¾ cup crumbs)

½ cup bourbon

2 tablespoons tomato paste

1½ cups clam juice

2 cups heavy cream

Vegetable oil, for frying

All-purpose flour, for dredging

1 large egg, lightly beaten

2 chipotle chiles in adobo, seeded and minced

3 tablespoons fresh lime juice

2 teaspoons chopped fresh thyme

8 to 12 gingersnaps, for serving

SERVES 4 TO 6

Okay, I know I'm getting a little fancy, but I used this recipe for an *Iron Chef America* battle (the episode aired on December 2, 2012) where ya have to BRING it! Gingersnaps and gingerbread were the secret ingredients. I ground up the gingersnaps, dredged and rolled the swimmerets in the snaps, then fried and pulverized 'em to make a luscious topping. The outcome was surprisingly delicious! I didn't win, but if I'd had a vote, this dish should have put me over the top.

1 Put 2 inches of water in a large pot, add salt, and bring to a boil. Add the lobsters, head first, cover, and boil over high heat until the lobsters are bright red all over and the antennae pull out easily, about 8 minutes. Transfer the lobsters to a large rimmed baking sheet and let cool.

2 Working over a large, wide bowl to catch all of the juices, pull the tails from the bodies and transfer the light green tamale (pulled from the body) to a small bowl. With scissors, cut the tail-end flippers from the tail and push to force the tail meat out of the top of the shell. Reserve the tail shells. Twist the claws from the bodies, and working over the bowl, break the claws from the legs or knuckles, and pull the thin claws back and forth to release the juices in the large part of the claws. With a nutcracker, crack the claws and knuckles to remove the meat. Reserve or freeze the bodies for another use. Put the meat in the bowl with the tamale and refrigerate. Pour any juice from the baking sheet into the bowl of lobster juices. You should have about 1½ cups of lobster juices. Pull off the little swimmer feet from the undersides of the lobster tails and reserve. Pat them dry with paper towels. Let stand on the paper towels to air-dry.

3   In a large pot, heat the olive oil. Add the carrots, cover, and cook over medium heat for 3 minutes. Add the onion and ginger, season with salt and pepper, cover, and cook over medium-low heat, stirring a few times, until softened, about 8 minutes. Add the mushrooms, cover, and cook over medium-high heat, stirring a few times, until the mushrooms are tender and lightly browned, about 5 minutes. Stir in ½ cup of the ground gingersnaps.

4   Have a long-handled match ready by the stove, then carefully pour in the bourbon. Light the match and stand back as you flambé the bourbon. It will flame intensely for about 20 seconds and then die down. Stir in the tomato paste, then the clam juice and reserved lobster juices until smooth. Simmer, partially covered, over medium-low heat, stirring often, until thickened, about 5 minutes. Stir in the heavy cream and simmer about 5 minutes longer, stirring a few times. Discard the ginger slices.

5   In a medium saucepan, heat ½ inch of vegetable oil to 325°F. Add the dried swimmerets and cook until crisp, about 1 minute. Stand back to avoid any splatter. With a slotted spoon, drain the swimmerets on paper towels and season with salt.

6   Remove the saucepan from the heat while you bread the swimmerets. Put flour in a shallow dish. Put the beaten egg in a small bowl and put the remaining ¼ cup of ground gingersnaps in another small bowl. Dredge half the swimmerets in the flour and then dip into the egg, allowing excess egg to drip off. Coat the swimmerets in the ground gingersnaps. Repeat with the remaining swimmerets.

7   Return the saucepan of oil to medium-low heat and heat to 300°F. Add half the swimmerets and fry until browned, about 40 seconds. With a slotted spoon, drain on paper towels and repeat with the remaining swimmerets. Season with salt and let cool completely. Transfer the fried swimmerets to a spice grinder and grind to a powder.

8   Stir the chipotles and lime juice into the bisque. Chop the reserved lobster meat into bite-size pieces and add to the bisque along with the reserved tamale and thyme. Season with salt and pepper and simmer for 1 or 2 minutes to heat through. Ladle the bisque into bowls, sprinkle with the swimmeret powder, and serve with gingersnaps.

The bisque can be made ahead and refrigerated for up to 2 days. Reheat gently. The swimmerets can be fried up to 1 hour in advance. Keep uncovered at room temperature and pulverize just before adding to the bisque.

DR. KLAW'S LOBSTAH ROLLS

There is nothing fancy about a lobster roll. They were invented on the side of the road. I see a lot of overly dressed-up lobster rolls in restaurants with garnishes and beds of lettuce, too much mayo, and way too many odd green bits mixed in with the lobster. I hate lettuce and celery in my lobster roll! Lobster rolls should taste like lobster, not celery! Just use a good sweet hot-dog bun, big chunks of lobster, a little mayo, and some butter and you will have perfection. I think my secret is steaming the lobster in a salty bath . . . and never tossing out the lobster liquids that are in the shells. Save every last drop. That liquid is like lobster extract . . . or lobster flavor on steroids. It's why some people refer to my roll as a Dr. Klaw Crack Roll. Trust Dr. Klaw on this one!

1 large onion, halved

2 tablespoons coarse sea salt

4 large garlic cloves, smashed and peeled

3 bay leaves

1 teaspoon black peppercorns, cracked

4 (1½-pound) lobsters

8 tablespoons (1 stick) salted butter

1 teaspoon garlic powder

6 top-sliced hot dog buns

2 tablespoons mayonnaise

Fine sea salt

Old Bay seasoning

SERVES 6

1   In a large clam or lobster pot, add 2 inches of water. Put in the onion halves cut sides down and add the coarse sea salt, garlic, bay leaves, and black peppercorns. Bring to a boil over high heat.

2   Put in the lobsters head up, the first 2 sitting on the onion halves, and loosely stack the other 2 lobsters, making sure all the lobsters are evenly spaced apart. Cover and cook over medium-high heat until bright red all over, about 6 minutes. They will be a little undercooked for a reason!

3   Transfer the lobsters to a large rimmed baking sheet and let cool. Work over the sheet to collect all the lobster juices and fat. Twist the tails and the claws from the bodies. Pull off the tail ends or flippers from the tail shells and push the tail meat out of the shells with your thumb. Cut down the top of the tails and discard the dark vein. Twist the knuckles from the claws. Cover the claws with a kitchen towel and, with a mallet or the back of a large knife, gently crack the claws on both sides to loosen the shells from the meat. Break the shell off of the claws and pull out the meat, preferably in one piece. Break up the knuckles and push out the meat.

4   Cut the tails down the center and give all of the lobster meat just a few chops; the meat should be in nice chunks. You should have about 5 cups of meat. Put the meat and the collected juices in a large skillet and set aside.

5   Now heat a griddle. Meanwhile, in a small saucepan, melt the butter with the garlic powder and stir. Open the hot dog buns and brush only the insides with some of the garlic butter. Toast the buns on the hot griddle on medium-high heat until golden brown and crisp, about 2 minutes per side. Reduce the heat to medium if the griddle gets too hot.

6   Very gently reheat the lobster meat over low heat until barely hot. Remove the skillet from the heat, stir in the mayonnaise, and season with fine sea salt. Pack the lobster meat into the toasted buns and drizzle each with a little more of the garlic butter. Sprinkle with Old Bay seasoning and serve right away. You should have a nice pink-orange sauce developing around the meat as a result of the mayo and lobster juice cooking just a bit.

The cooked lobster meat and juices can be refrigerated overnight. Bring to room temperature, then reheat very gently if you are assembling the rolls the following day. Save the lobster bodies and shells for bisque or stock. Store in the freezer for up to 1 month.

Lobster rolls should taste like lobster, not celery! Just use a good sweet hot-dog bun, big chunks of lobster, a little mayo, and some butter and you will have perfection.

LOBSTER & SMOKED CHICKEN PAELLA

My brother-in-law Matt is a tyrant in the kitchen. I don't get within ten feet of him when he's behind the stove. If my sister, who is a devoted and loving wife, approaches him when he is in his martial arts cooking trance, he will growl, "Greta, can't you see I'm cooking?" Also, there is no such thing as cooking one-two-three with him. It has to take all day or to him it's not really cooking. Then, if his paella turns out perfect—and every one I have tasted always does—you have to listen to him go on and on. Matt still talks about a particular paella he did a few years ago that turned out even better than any other. You know what? I can deal with it, because it really was that good!

Don't be put off by the number of ingredients. You can feel free to omit any of the seafood you can't find. I include them all, because that's what a traditional Spanish paella does. It's a way to use a lot of ingredients in one pot and it's traditionally served family style.

Sea salt

2 (1¼-pound) lobsters

3 cups clam juice

3 cups chicken stock

½ teaspoon saffron threads

1 cup hardwood chips, soaked in water for 30 minutes and drained (optional)

3 tablespoons olive oil

¾ pound smoked, spicy sausage such as andouille or chorizo (not dried), sliced ½ inch thick

1 large onion, cut into medium dice

4 garlic cloves, minced

½ teaspoon smoked sweet paprika, plus more for sprinkling

2 cups medium- to small-grain Spanish rice, such as Bomba, Calasparra, or Valencia

Salt and freshly ground black pepper

½ (7-ounce) jar piquillo peppers, with their liquid, peppers thinly sliced

Chicken pieces from a smoked or slow-grilled chicken, preferably 2 drumsticks, 2 thighs, and 2 wings; if using breast meat slice 1 inch thick and add to paella with the lobster meat

1 dozen littleneck clams, scrubbed

2 dozen mussels, scrubbed

¾ pound large shrimp, in the shell

¾ pound small squid, bodies sliced crosswise ½ inch thick, tentacles whole

1 cup frozen peas, thawed

2 tablespoons chopped fresh flat-leaf parsley

Lemon wedges, for serving

SERVES 6

(recipe continues)

1 In a large pot, add 2 inches of water and 2 to 3 tablespoons of sea salt. Bring to a boil and add the lobsters head first. Cover and steam until bright red all over, and almost cooked through, about 6 minutes. Transfer the lobsters to a large rimmed baking sheet and let cool. Twist the claws from the lobster bodies and crack all over with the back of a heavy knife or a nutcracker. Remove the tails from the bodies and lay them flat on a cutting board. Cut down the center to split the tails and keep the meat in the shell. Discard the dark vein. Refrigerate the lobster pieces.

2 Light a gas grill. Put the clam juice and chicken stock in a saucepan and crumble in ¼ teaspoon of the saffron. On the grill or on a stove, cover and bring to a simmer over medium heat. Turn off the burner and keep warm. If using, put the drained hardwood chips in a packet of heavy-duty foil and punch holes in it.

3 Set a 17-inch paella pan over 2 gas grill burners on medium high-heat. Add 2 tablespoons of olive oil and the sausage and cook, stirring a few times, until browned, about 5 minutes. With a slotted spoon, transfer the sausage to a medium bowl. Add the onion and cook, stirring, for 1 minute. Stir in the garlic, cover the grill, and cook, stirring a few times, until softened, about 8 minutes. Stir in the smoked paprika and the remaining ¼ teaspoon of saffron and cook for 1 minute. Stir in the rice and the remaining 1 tablespoon of olive oil, season with salt and pepper, and stir to coat the rice with the oil and flavorings. Stir in the piquillo peppers and liquid and 4 cups of the warm saffron stock. If using, put the foil packet of wood chips over part of the grill burner, just so it smokes slowly, then cover the grill. The cover should come down on the pan and cover most of it, but it can stick out a bit. Cook for 10 minutes without stirring.

4 Again, without stirring, rotate the pan and shake a few times and add ½ cup of the saffron stock. Poke the sausage and chicken pieces, clams, and mussels, hinged sides down, in the rice. Cover and cook for 5 minutes. Drizzle 1 cup of the saffron stock in the pan around the edges and where there may be a thinner and drier layer of rice. Adjust the heat to medium if the rice in any part of the pan starts to get too dark. But continue not to stir.

5 If using, move the foil packet of wood chips to another part of a burner to burn them evenly. Arrange the shrimp and squid in the rice, rotate the pan, cover, and cook for 5 minutes. Drizzle the remaining ½ cup of saffron stock over the rice. Scatter in the peas over the rice and arrange the lobster pieces in the rice. Cover and cook over medium heat for about 10 minutes. Check the bottom of the pan to see how dark the rice is in spots. Dark brown, crisp rice from the bottom of the pan is a treat the Spanish love. Do not burn the rice, though. If you see that the rice is not brown, raise the heat to high and cook for another minute or so.

6 Remove the paella pan from the grill, cover with a clean kitchen towel, and let stand for 10 minutes. Sprinkle with the parsley and some smoked paprika and serve with lemon wedges.

The steamed lobsters can be refrigerated overnight.

Cuban GRILLED LOBSTER TAILS
WITH GARLIC-CURRY BUTTER & RUM

5 tablespoons unsalted butter, softened

2 garlic cloves, minced

½ teaspoon curry powder

Hot sauce, such as Frank's

Salt and freshly ground black pepper

4 (10-ounce) lobster tails in the shell

Vegetable oil

Dark rum, for splashing

SERVES 4

Grilling lobster is not difficult, but some guests prefer not to witness the act, so you can send them off for a few drinks in another room and tell them you'll let them know when it's over. Lobsters are living creatures so I believe in killing them the fastest, most humane way possible. Lobster tails cook quickly, so when in doubt, take them off the grill sooner rather than later. Lots of people will boil or steam a lobster before grilling it ... but take it from my Cuban friends in Miami who inspired this recipe. ¡No se necesita!

1   In a small bowl, blend together the butter, garlic, and curry powder. Add a few dashes of hot sauce and season with salt and pepper.

2   With scissors, cut down the center of the lobster tail shells on the top side and discard the dark intestinal vein. Loosen the meat from the shells and rub it with oil. Season the lobster lightly with salt and pepper.

3   Light a grill. Grill the lobster tails over a medium-hot fire, meaty side down, until light grill marks appear, about 2 minutes. Turn the lobster tails and spread each with about 1 teaspoon of the butter. Turn the lobster meaty side down again and grill until golden brown, about 2 minutes. Turn the lobster tails shell side down and splash with some rum. Add more butter, but not all of it, to the lobster tails—poking it in the shell under the meat and on top—and let cook until the lobster releases juice and starts simmering, about 3 minutes. The lobster tails will continue to lose translucency until a thin band remains down the center of the tails; this should take about 3 minutes longer. Just before removing from the grill, spread the tails with the remaining butter. Serve right away.

MUSSELS

One reason I love mussels, apart from the fact that they taste so good, is that compared to oysters and clams they are easy to gather. Instead of having to dig around in the sand, the way you do with clams, you can find mussels right out in the open. It's not even remotely a fair fight between man and mussel, especially when the tide goes out, exposing acres of them. Well before I had eaten my first mussel, I used to gather them with my dad, crack 'em open, and dump them in our little creek. This attracted lots of hungry minnows and crabs. I had hours and hours of entertainment watching the minnows and crabs fighting over crushed mussels.

I also loved watching the crafty gulls feed on mussels. They would grab a mussel in their beak and then, riding the updrafts from the waves, hover about twenty feet over the dunes. When they were lined up with a nice big rock near the water's edge, they'd drop the mussel on the rock. It would crack open, and in that way, the gulls got to the meat of the matter without a lot of effort. That particular rock near my family's house on Cape Cod must be absolutely perfect for mussel cracking because generations of gulls have been using it for the same trick all my life.

There are a couple kinds of mussels where I come from: shiny black and ridged. Some people say that the ridged mussels are not safe for consumption. But I once served them at a party and everyone lived to tell the story. . . . My dad, who is an expert in these matters, says they are unsafe when there is a red tide (which carries dangerous microbes), but so is a lot of other seafood. I use both kinds of mussels, but fish stores and restaurants always serve the shiny black ones. Mussels are good in any soup, chowder, stew, or paella-like dish as a way to fill them out with more seafood that is plentiful. Even if you don't gather them yourself, they aren't costly. Don't forget to debeard them if you do gather them yourself.

MUSSEL SOUP WITH SAFFRON & LEEKS

From the Full Disclosure Department: I didn't make this seafood recipe when I was by the sea. I was in Vermont with Gabi (my friend and the photographer of this book), who was dubious about trying ocean fare in a landlocked state. I had to convince her that I had a connection to someone who could get fresher ingredients than her Martha's Vineyard go-to guy. So looking out at the Green Mountains, I threw this dish together and Gabi conceded that it was the best mussel recipe ever made in the Green Mountains. I think that was a compliment.

½ cup dry white wine

1 bay leaf

2 pounds mussels

3 tablespoons unsalted butter

1 large leek, white and light green parts, thinly sliced

⅛ teaspoon saffron threads, crumbled

1 large ripe plum tomato, finely chopped

¼ pound green beans, cut into ½-inch pieces

1 tablespoon brandy or Pernod

½ cup heavy cream

Salt and freshly ground black pepper

Small buttered croutons, for serving

SERVES 4

1 In a large saucepan, combine 1 cup of water, the wine, and the bay leaf and bring to a boil. Add the mussels, cover, and cook over medium-high heat, shaking the pan a few times, until the mussels open, about 4 minutes. Discard the bay leaf and any mussels that do not open. With a slotted spoon, transfer the mussels to a large bowl. Pour the mussel broth into a 2-cup glass measure, leaving any grit at the bottom of the pan. Remove the mussels from the shells, cover, and keep in the fridge.

2 In a clean saucepan, melt the butter. Add the leek, cover, and cook over medium-low heat, stirring a few times, until soft, about 5 minutes. Add the saffron threads, tomato, and green beans, cover, and cook until the tomato dissolves, about 5 minutes. Add the brandy and cook for 1 minute. Add the 2 cups of mussel broth and the cream, cover, and simmer over low heat until the flavors blend, about 5 minutes. Add the mussels and simmer gently 1 to 2 minutes, to reheat. Season with salt and pepper. Ladle into bowls and top with croutons.

The soup can be refrigerated overnight, either in advance or as leftovers.

MUSSELS IN THAI RED CURRY

2 tablespoons vegetable oil

3 garlic cloves, minced

2 medium shallots, thinly sliced

3 tablespoons, packed, palm sugar or light brown sugar

1½ tablespoons Thai red curry paste

1 tablespoon finely grated lime zest

5 tablespoons fish sauce

¼ cup fresh lime juice

3 stalks lemongrass, lower third of stalks, cut into 1-inch lengths and smashed

1 cup unsweetened coconut milk

Freshly ground black pepper

3 pounds mussels, scrubbed

3 to 4 cups steamed rice or about ½ pound cooked rice noodles, for serving

½ cup chopped fresh cilantro

SERVES 4

I have been making this dish for years. This is the recipe I used on Cape Cod when my guests were fearful I was serving poison mussels. Turned out they loved the ridged mussels that they all thought they were going to die from. In my mind it's okay to eat them. I love a version of this (made with shiny black, not ridged mussels) that's served at Flex Mussels in New York. It's my favorite place for mussels, in part because the family who owns it is from the great mussel-producing area of Prince Edward Island.

1 In a large pot, heat the oil. Add the garlic and shallots and cook over medium heat until golden, about 3 minutes. Add the sugar and cook, stirring, until caramelized, about 1 minute. Add the curry paste and lime zest and cook, stirring, until fragrant, about 1 minute. Stir in the fish sauce, lime juice, lemongrass, and coconut milk and bring to a boil. Grind in the black pepper.

2 Add the mussels, cover, and cook over medium-high heat, shaking the pot a few times, until the mussels open, about 4 minutes. Discard any that do not open.

3 Put the rice or rice noodles in 4 shallow bowls. Spoon the mussels and sauce over, sprinkle with the cilantro, and serve.

MUSSELS *Fra Diavolo*
WITH ROASTED GARLIC

I always wondered who this guy Fra Diavolo was. A monk named after the devil? It never made sense to me. Then I learned that the "devil" part of the name refers to fiery-hot chile flakes. The roasted garlic contributes a sweet nutty taste. Mussels give off so much sweet liquid that it's easy to steam them or flavor the liquid in all kinds of ways.

2 large heads garlic, top quarter cut off

6 tablespoons olive oil

Salt and freshly ground black pepper

1 bunch scallions, finely chopped

1 teaspoon chile flakes or 1 habanero chile, finely chopped

3 large plum tomatoes, finely chopped

¾ cup dry white wine

4 pounds mussels, scrubbed

½ cup chopped fresh basil or flat-leaf parsley

Toasted baguette slices, for serving

SERVES 6

1   Preheat the oven to 350°F. Put the garlic in a small baking dish, cut sides up, and drizzle the cut sides of the garlic with 1 tablespoon of the olive oil, then season with salt and pepper. Cover and bake for about 1 hour, until very soft. Squeeze the soft garlic from the papery skins into a small bowl. Stir in 2 tablespoons of the olive oil and season with salt and pepper.

2   In a large pot, heat the remaining 3 tablespoons of olive oil. Add the scallions and chile flakes, and cook over medium heat for 2 minutes. Add the tomatoes, cover, and cook until the tomatoes dissolve, about 4 minutes. Raise the heat to medium-high and add the garlic puree and the wine.

3   Bring the scallion-garlic mixture to a boil and add the mussels. Cover and cook, shaking the pot a few times, until the mussels open, about 5 minutes. With a large slotted spoon or Chinese wire strainer, lift the open mussels from the pot and transfer to serving bowls. Discard any mussels that do not open.

4   Remove the pot from the heat. Season the sauce with salt and pepper and add the basil. Pour the sauce over the mussels and serve right away with toasted baguette slices.

OCTOPUS

Once you own something as a pet, it's hard to eat one. I had a pet octopus when I lived in my first Brooklyn apartment. I kept him in a tank and we'd stare at each other for hours, just trying to figure the other guy out. One sad and fateful day, my octo up and left me (was it something I said?); he crept out of his tank and scuttled across a few blocks, heading down to the East River. The evidence? A week after the great escape, a teacher friend sent me one of his student's essays detailing an escaped octo on Bedford Avenue making a run for the river.

That wasn't the only time an octopus got the best of me. There was the octopus I challenged off Catalina Island. I was snorkeling and came across an octopus in a pipe five or six feet down. He taunted me with one tentacle by sticking it out of the pipe just long enough for me to grab hold; I would yank and he would retreat, grasping onto the rocks inside the pipe. I didn't have the lung capacity to keep fighting, and I would rush to the surface gasping for air and yelling profanities. He was playing me, I knew it, and he won every time.

In the battle of Ben vs. Octopus, it is, at best, a split decision. In Hawaii, I was diving for them and an old-timer told me I had to bite them on the head to kill them fast and heroically. I had no intention of doing so until one ornery octopus started coming at my neck like a boa constrictor. In a panic, I did just as the old-timer told me and bit down hard, right between the eyes, and sure enough it worked—and maybe saved my life!

AGUADILLA OCTOPUS
WITH CONCH IN RAISIN SAUCE

Aguadilla, Puerto Rico, is a beautiful town on the northwest coast where I rent a little beach shack. There is always octopus for sale right where the boats pull up onto the beach. A local chef there showed me the neat trick of finishing the boiling/tenderizing part of octopus prep with fifteen minutes of boiling in red wine, for great purple color and wonderful flavor. I'm glad I learned something that night because romantically it was a bust.

1½ pounds octopus tentacles (3 tentacles)

2 cups dry red wine

3 tablespoons olive oil, plus more for drizzling

1 pound cleaned conch, pounded

1 quart coconut water

1 large onion, cut into ½-inch dice

1 large red bell pepper, cored, seeded, and cut into ½-inch dice

1 large green bell pepper, cored, seeded, and cut into ½-inch dice

2 garlic cloves, minced

1 teaspoon adobo seasoning powder

2 tablespoons dark raisins

1 cup tomato sauce

1 cup whole milk

Salt and freshly ground black pepper

Habanero hot sauce

1 pound large shrimp, in the shell

¼ cup chopped fresh cilantro

Cuban Yellow Rice (page 243) for serving

SERVES 6

1 Put the octopus tentacles in a large pot, cover with water, and bring to a boil. Simmer over low heat, skimming the surface a few times, until the octopus is tender, about 50 minutes. Drain the octopus and transfer to a medium saucepan. Add the red wine and ½ cup water and bring to a boil. Simmer over low heat, carefully turning a few times, for 15 minutes. With tongs, transfer the octopus to a large bowl and drizzle generously with olive oil, coating thoroughly.

2 Meanwhile, put the conch in a large saucepan and cover with the coconut water. Bring to a boil, then simmer over low heat, skimming the surface a few times, until tender, about 1 hour. Drain the conch and place in a medium bowl. Drizzle generously with olive oil and coat thoroughly.

3 While the octopus and conch are simmering, prepare the sofrito-raisin sauce. In a large saucepan, heat the 3 tablespoons of olive oil. Add the onion, the red and green bell peppers, and the garlic, and cook, partially covered over low heat, stirring occasionally, until very soft, about 30 minutes. Add the adobo seasoning and raisins and cook, stirring, for 1 minute. Add the tomato sauce and simmer for a few minutes to blend the flavors. Add the milk and simmer for about 5 minutes. Season with salt and pepper and the hot sauce and remove from the heat.

4 Light a grill. Drizzle the shrimp with olive oil and season with salt and pepper. Season the octopus tentacles and the conch with salt and pepper. Grill the seafood together over a medium-hot fire. Grill the octopus until nicely charred and crisp, about 5 minutes on the first side and about 3 minutes on the other side. Grill the conch about 2 minutes per side. Grill the shrimp about 2 minutes per side. Transfer the octopus tentacles and the conch to a carving board and let rest for a minute or so. Cut the octopus and conch into thin slices.

5 Gently reheat the sauce and stir in the sliced octopus, conch, shrimp, and cilantro. Spoon the yellow rice into the center of each bowl. Spoon the seafood sauce around the rice and serve, passing more hot sauce at the table.

Grilled OCTOPUS GAZPACHO
WITH SHELL BEANS

Octopus

1½ pounds octopus tentacles

3 fennel stalks, thinly sliced

1 small onion, thinly sliced

½ cup dry white wine

1 bay leaf

Olive oil

Salt and freshly ground black pepper

Gazpacho

½ pound fresh shelled cranberry beans, or frozen and thawed

Olive oil

Salt and freshly ground black pepper

3 cups tomato juice

1 medium cucumber, peeled, halved, seeded, and cut into ¼-inch dice

1 yellow bell pepper, cored, seeded, and cut into ¼-inch dice

1 small sweet onion, cut into ¼-inch dice

1 fennel bulb, cored and cut into ¼-inch dice, stalks reserved

1 jalapeño, seeded and minced

1 scallion, thinly sliced

3 tablespoons chopped fresh cilantro

½ teaspoon finely grated lime zest

½ teaspoon finely grated lemon zest

1 tablespoon fresh lime juice

1 tablespoon fresh lemon juice

SERVES 4

I once grilled a sixteen-foot octopus in Brooklyn, probably setting some kind of Brooklyn octopus grilling record, but tragically, it was inedible. It was the chewiest thing imaginable. I couldn't figure out if it needed more or less grill time, and that's when I started to read up on boiling. Growing up eating octopus, I always thought the big challenge with octopus was overcooking it, the same way people overcook string beans. Wrong! For perfect results: First boil the octopus for a good long while, anywhere from a half hour to an hour, until it begins to feel tender. Where other seafood gets tough and dry when treated this way, octopus gets succulent and tender. Then, finish it on the grill for a nice crispy char.

1. To prepare the octopus: Put the octopus tentacles in a large pot and add the fennel, onion, wine, and bay leaf. Add enough water to cover and bring to a boil. Simmer over low heat, skimming the surface a few times, until the octopus is tender, about 45 minutes. Drain the octopus, drizzle with olive oil, and keep refrigerated.

2. To prepare the gazpacho: In a medium saucepan of boiling water, cook the beans until tender, about 12 minutes. Drain the beans and transfer to a medium bowl. Drizzle with olive oil and season with salt and pepper.

3. In a large bowl, combine the tomato juice with the cucumber, bell pepper, onion, fennel, jalapeño, scallion, and 1 tablespoon cilantro. Add the beans, cover, and refrigerate until thoroughly chilled, about 2 hours or overnight.

4. About 2 hours before serving, stir the lime and lemon zest and juice into the gazpacho and season with salt and pepper. Keep refrigerated.

5. Light a grill. Season the octopus with salt and pepper and grill over a medium-hot fire until nicely charred and crisp, about 5 minutes per side. Transfer the octopus to a carving board and let rest for a few minutes.

6. Ladle the gazpacho into shallow bowls. Slice the octopus crosswise about ½ inch wide. Cut the slices into ½-inch pieces and add to the gazpacho. Garnish with the remaining 2 tablespoons of cilantro and serve.

Without the lime and lemon zest and juice, the gazpacho can be refrigerated overnight.

OCTOBALLS

I sort of made these on the Food Network show *Chopped*. By that, I mean I made 'em in a rush, then I got chopped. No love! I am not a super-fast restaurant cook. My bet is neither are most of you. But you don't have to worry about starting a fire on prime time television like I did, or cooking and plating this entire dish in under fifteen minutes. Anyway, these balls are delicious and people still seem to have a good time making snarky jokes about my octoballs. Eat 'em and weep! They ARE that good!

Precooked octopus tentacles can be purchased in Japanese or Korean markets.

½ pound cooked octopus, cut into ¼-inch dice

2 tablespoons minced onion

1 tablespoon chopped fresh flat-leaf parsley

3 tablespoons mayonnaise

¼ pound medium shrimp, shelled, deveined, and minced

1 large egg

¼ teaspoon salt

¼ teaspoon freshly ground black pepper

1 teaspoon soy sauce

¼ cup plus 2 tablespoons panko bread crumbs

Vegetable oil, for frying

1 tablespoon rice vinegar

1 teaspoon Sriracha sauce

Bonito flakes, for garnish (optional)

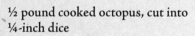

MAKES 12 BALLS;
serves 4

1 In a large bowl, combine the octopus, onion, parsley, 2 tablespoons mayonnaise, and the shrimp and blend well. In a small bowl, beat the egg and beat in the salt, pepper, and soy sauce. Stir the egg mixture into the octopus mixture until thoroughly combined, then fold in the panko. Form the mixture into 12 balls.

2 In a large cast-iron skillet, heat ¼ inch of oil until shimmering. Add the octoballs and cook over medium-high heat for 1 minute. Reduce the heat to medium, cover with a splatter screen, and cook, turning a few times, until the octoballs are browned all over and cooked through, about 6 minutes total time. Transfer the octoballs to paper towels to drain.

3 Meanwhile, in a small bowl, blend together the remaining 1 tablespoon of mayonnaise with the vinegar and Sriracha. Put the octoballs on a platter, drizzle the mayonnaise mixture over them, sprinkle with the bonito flakes, if using, and serve.

OYSTERS

I grew up with oysters and oyster fanatics, but I was not one of those kids who fell in love with them at a young age. In fact, like most kids, I found them kind of disgusting, to be honest. When I threw back my first oyster, instead of the pleasurable experience I anticipated, I found it way too intense and super-slimy. Our New England oyster is very briny, and very big. So it's a lot of oyster for your first one!

Graduating from those first oysters, it was an easy jump to milder West Coast oysters and the super-mild and buttery tropical oysters of the Gulf Coast. My earlier education tasting oysters of Wellfleet on Cape Cod has served me well in learning to slurp down and actually enjoy the many varieties of oyster I have come across in my travels. For my money, nothing compares to those Wellfleets. We should pat ourselves on the back. Although we can unpat ourselves for harvesting so many oysters for export that we had to bring up oysters from the South to reseed our decimated oyster beds.

Years after learning to enjoy raw oysters, I discovered that cooking them can be wonderful, too; they're great in pan roasts and fried. My new favorite is to grill them, let the top pop open, and eat 'em right out of the shell, a mini bowl of chowder. Some hard-core New England oystermen might be rolling over in their graves at the mention of cooking their beloved oyster . . . but I'm not afraid of ghosts.

If you are concerned about the environment, it is comforting to know that farmed oysters—which is what so many of the commercially available oysters are these days—filter and clean the waters of the shallows and bays where they are raised. So not only are they 100 percent sustainable, they actually are performing a valuable service when you reintroduce them to a body of water.

OYSTER PAN ROAST
WITH GARLIC BUTTER TOASTS

Oysters, cream, and some seasonings are all you need for a perfect pan roast. But you have to open the oysters and save all their juice (in fancy talk, that juice is known as liquor). Depending on their shape and the wave of their shells, oysters can be either easy to open or impossible. That is why this recipe is for two people; you only have to shuck a dozen oysters. If you have another set of willing hands to open more oysters, you can double the recipe.

2 tablespoons unsalted butter, softened

1 garlic clove, minced

1 tablespoon chopped fresh flat-leaf parsley

Salt and freshly ground black pepper

½ cup light cream

12 medium-size oysters, shucked, oyster liquor reserved (about ⅓ cup)

1 teaspoon Worcestershire sauce

2 slices of light, crisp Italian or Portuguese bread, toasted and halved

Tabasco or other sharp hot sauce

SERVES 2

1 In a small bowl, blend the butter with the garlic and parsley and season with salt and pepper.

2 In a medium skillet, combine the cream, oyster liquor, and Worcestershire sauce and bring to a gentle simmer over low heat. Add the oysters and cook just until their edges curl, about 1½ minutes.

3 Meanwhile, spread half the garlic butter on the hot toasts and put 2 halves in each shallow bowl for serving. Add a dash of hot sauce to the oyster roast and pour into the bowls, over the toasts. Top with the remaining garlic butter and serve right away.

CORNMEAL FRIED OYSTERS
WITH ASPARAGUS SALAD

I am big-time into cold salads with a warm component, especially a crispy warm component. The grittiness of cornmeal pairs so well with the creamy brininess of oysters. When asparagus hits the farmer's market in the spring and the local fishermen bring in their haul of oysters, I can't wait to make this salad every year to mark the official end of winter and the beginning of spring. This is also a good time to pick fiddlehead ferns, which work well as a seasonal side dish or as a substitute for the asparagus. I just sauté them in butter.

Salt

1 pound thick asparagus, trimmed

3½ tablespoons olive oil

4 paper-thin slices prosciutto

1 small shallot, minced

1 small garlic clove, minced

1½ tablespoons white wine vinegar

1 teaspoon Dijon mustard

1 teaspoon chopped fresh tarragon

Freshly ground black pepper

Vegetable oil, for frying

2 large eggs, beaten with 1 tablespoon water

½ cup fine cornmeal

24 medium-size shucked oysters

2 cups baby lettuce leaves

10 cherry tomatoes, halved

SERVES 4

1   In a large skillet of boiling, salted water, cook the asparagus until just tender, about 4 minutes. Drain and spread out the asparagus on a large rimmed baking sheet to cool. Pat dry and cut the asparagus into 1-inch lengths.

2   Wipe out the skillet and heat ½ tablespoon of the olive oil. Add the prosciutto and cook over medium-high heat until crisp, about 1 minute. Drain and when cool, tear the prosciutto into pieces.

3   In a small bowl, combine the shallot, garlic, and vinegar and let stand for 5 minutes. Stir in the mustard, the remaining 3 tablespoons of olive oil, and the tarragon and season with salt and pepper.

4   Preheat the oven to 350°F. In a large saucepan, heat 2 inches of vegetable oil to 370°F. Have a large baking sheet with a few layers of paper towels near the stove. Put the paper towels on half of the baking sheet, leaving the other half bare. Put the eggs with water in a shallow bowl. Put the cornmeal in another shallow bowl and season with salt and pepper. Working with 6 oysters at a time, dip the oysters in the egg mixture, letting excess drip off. Dredge the oysters in the cornmeal and add to the hot oil. Fry the oysters, turning once, until golden brown and crisp, about 1 minute. With a slotted spoon, quickly drain the oysters on the paper towels, then push them to the bare side. Repeat with the remaining oysters. Put the oysters in the oven for a minute while you dress the salad.

5   In a large bowl, combine the asparagus, prosciutto, lettuce, and tomatoes. Add the dressing and toss well. Divide the salad among 4 shallow bowls. Top with the fried oysters and serve.

Grilled POP-UP OYSTERS

I have tested this recipe on surfers at my home break in the Rockaways. For you nonsurfers, a home break is your local surf spot, and for you non—New Yorkers, Rockaway is on the coast of Queens. Good thing is surfers are very honest critics. Bad thing is they are so hungry after a surf session they might eat anything, so I don't know how much their honesty counts. My friends would probably eat clamshells and come back for seconds.

This recipe is great for those times when you don't feel like struggling to open oysters. Face it, some oysters and clams just refuse to open with a knife, but throw them on the grill and they will open up all by themselves. POP! Top this with herbed Tabasco butter and eat while standing around the grill. It's so simple and fun but it will blow your mind with flavor. If you don't have oysters, this works just as well with clams.

3 tablespoons unsalted butter, softened

1 small shallot, minced

2 teaspoons chopped fresh sage

1 tablespoon minced fresh chives

1 teaspoon dry sherry or brandy

1 teaspoon sharp hot sauce such as Tabasco

Salt and freshly ground black pepper

6 medium-size oysters

SERVES 2

1 In a small bowl, blend together the butter, shallot, sage, chives, sherry, and hot sauce and season with salt and pepper.

2 Light a grill. Put the oysters, flat side up, over a hot fire and grill until the oysters pops open, 2 to 3 minutes. As they open, carefully transfer the oysters to a plate, keeping the juices in the shell. Take off the top shell, add a good dab of the butter mixture, and serve right away.

SCALLOPS

Scallops are amazing little animals. Using a jet under their shell, they go "teeuh teeuh teeuh" and are able to zip through the water. It's kind of cartoonish and totally wild. There's that jet propulsion, that beautiful shell, and those blue eyes on the perimeter of their shell that let them see 360 degrees (as my biologist dad told me when I was little). They can look at us humans from every angle, and I sometimes wondered, how can we, in good conscience, eat these little guys?

Simple. They are amazingly delicious!

My favorite way to eat them is raw, with nothing on them. But, that doesn't make for a good cookbook recipe, does it? Okay, I really like 'em cooked, too! The best way to cook scallops is to do them lightly. For years, people traditionally cooked them all the way through, and that's why they took on that pungent smell and tennis-shoe texture. But now that we've learned how to cook them—with a super-light touch— they're so good. According to most chefs, the trick to cooking them is to not move them once they hit the pan. That way, a crust builds up, whereas if you move them you break the crust and the water seeps out of them and produces a boring, dry scallop.

Cast iron is the only way to go because you need a pan that gets hot all over and holds the heat. Then you just sear them for a short while. The cast iron has to be oiled so the scallops release easily, retaining their golden crust.

There are two kinds of scallops: bay scallops and sea scallops. They are the same animal, but the bay scallops are smaller and sweeter. Sea scallops can cook a little longer, so they develop a crust before getting too chewy from overcooking.

SCALLOP SANGRITA SOUP

The Mexican refreshment sangrita is a combination of tomato and orange juices that come together to form a new flavor of their own. It is a great background note for the succulent sweetness of scallops. Here, the scallops are seared in a hot cast-iron skillet. If you're in the mood for an extra kick, add a little tequila. I'm often in the mood.

1 ear of corn, shucked

2 pounds ripe tomatoes, cored and chopped

¾ cup fresh orange juice

1 tablespoon fresh lime juice

¾ teaspoon mild chile powder such as ancho

½ teaspoon hot chile powder such as New Mexico or Colorado

½ tablespoon grenadine syrup

Salt and freshly ground pepper

1¼ pounds sea scallops

2 tablespoons vegetable oil

4 to 6 black oil-cured olives, pitted and sliced

Splashes of tequila (optional)

SERVES 4 OR 6
as an appetizer or side

1 In a medium saucepan of boiling water, cook the ear of corn until just tender, about 3 minutes. Drain, cool, and cut the kernels from the cob.

2 In a food processor, puree the tomatoes. Pass the tomatoes through a fine strainer set over a large bowl to yield about 3½ cups of juice. Stir in the orange juice, lime juice, ancho chile powder, New Mexico chile powder, and grenadine, and season with salt and pepper. Cover and refrigerate until chilled, about 15 minutes or up to 6 hours.

3 Heat a large cast-iron skillet. Season the scallops with salt and pepper. Add half of the oil to the hot skillet and when shimmering, add half of the scallops. Cook over medium-high heat until richly browned, about 2 minutes. Turn the scallops and cook about 1 minute longer until barely cooked through. Transfer the scallops to a large plate and repeat with the remaining oil and scallops. Cut the scallops in half or in quarters and reserve any juices.

4 Ladle the soup into bowls and top with olive slices. Divide the scallops and their juices among the bowls. Add a splash of tequila, if you like, and serve.

SCALLOP CEVICHE

This recipe goes a long way toward proving my point that scallops are best served raw. Nothing is better than opening up the shell and popping those scallops in your mouth. The Japanese know this, and so do the Peruvians. Feel free to add popcorn before serving to give a little crunch to this dish. That's a super Peruvian-inspired idea because they love adding the giant toasted corn kernels they call *choclo* to almost everything.

1 cup diced sweet onion, rinsed and drained

¼ cup olive oil

2 tablespoons thick, unsweetened coconut milk, skimmed from the top of the can

Pinch of sugar

1 jalapeño, minced

½ habanero chile, seeded and very thinly sliced

1 teaspoon finely grated tangerine zest

¼ cup plus 2 tablespoons fresh tangerine juice

½ teaspoon finely grated lime zest

¼ cup plus 2 tablespoons fresh lime juice

Salt and freshly ground black pepper

1 pound sea scallops, cut into ¾-inch pieces

¼ cup chopped fresh cilantro

Small crisp lettuce leaves, such as Bibb, for garnish

SERVES 4 TO 6

1 In a large bowl, combine the onion, olive oil, coconut milk, sugar, jalapeño, habanero, tangerine zest and juice, and lime zest and juice, and season with salt and pepper.

2 Add the scallops and blend thoroughly. Cover and refrigerate the scallops for at least 2 hours or up to 4 hours, until the scallops are white on the outside and flavorful from the marinade. Taste a scallop to see if it has absorbed the flavors and has a slightly firm texture that means it has partially "cooked" in the marinade.

3 Check for salt and pepper and fold in the cilantro. Serve in small bowls garnished with lettuce leaves.

FRIED SCALLOPS

Sometimes I'm in the mood to re-create those awesome fried golden scallop nuggets I have loved my whole life at a seaside clam shack—actually one particular, teeny tiny shack: The Bite in the town of Menemsha on Martha's Vineyard stands out. I have tried and tried to get their method right. Finally, after many efforts, here is the closest I have come to crunchy golden fried scallops without having a mega-deep fryer. The nice thing about doing it yourself is that there is no line of tourists ahead of you, and no seagulls dive-bombing overhead. Once I was there when a wild skunk hung around my feet looking for scraps! These scallops are best served while gathered around the stove and eaten just as soon as they come out of the pan.

½ cup corn flour

½ cup all-purpose flour

1 teaspoon freshly ground black pepper

½ to 1 teaspoon cayenne pepper

1 teaspoon salt

2 cups milk

1 pound medium sea scallops, about 1 inch wide (large scallops halved)

Vegetable oil, for frying

Lemon wedges

Tartar sauce

SERVES 3 TO 4

1 In a large, shallow bowl, whisk together the corn flour, all-purpose flour, black pepper, cayenne pepper, and salt. In a medium bowl, combine the milk and scallops and stir well.

2 In a large saucepan, heat 2 inches of oil to 350°F. Set a rack for draining over a large rimmed baking sheet and place near the stove. Line half of it with paper towels. Also have ready a large handheld strainer or Chinese netted scoop. To fry the scallops in small batches, lift a handful of scallops from the milk and shake off excess. Drop the scallops into the flour mixture and shake the bowl to coat them thoroughly. Put the coated scallops in the strainer and shake over the bowl to remove excess coating. Add the scallops to the hot oil and let sit for about 20 seconds without moving them. Use a spoon to gently stir the scallops just to separate them. If they are moved too much the scallops' liquid might release. Fry for about 2 minutes, until golden brown and crisp.

3 Quickly drain the scallops on the paper-towel side of the rack, then push them to the other half of the rack. Repeat with the remaining scallops. Check the flour mixture and remove any lumps that may have formed before coating the next batch. Serve right away with lemon wedges and tartar sauce.

Jacques's SEARED SCALLOPS
WITH SWEET POTATO & MUSHROOMS

I ate this scallop dish at Palo Santo, a really chill restaurant in Park Slope run by Jacques Gautier. It's the ultimate farm-to-table place because he grows his own vegetables on the roof and even raises rabbits, which he cooks, too. One day, I dredged for scallops in Long Island and took them to Jacques, who threw this together soon after I walked through his door. One taste and I knew I was going to "steal" the recipe! But it turned out I didn't have to. Jacques was happy to be part of this book. Thanks, Jacques!

Sea salt

1 pound sweet potato, peeled and cut into 1-inch dice

¼ cup plus 2 tablespoons heavy cream

4 tablespoons (½ stick) unsalted butter

6 large sea scallops (live and in the shell), shucked, half the shells reserved

1 pound mixed wild mushrooms, stems trimmed, caps cut into quarters

Freshly ground black pepper

1 sprig fresh rosemary

¼ cup sherry

1 ounce pea shoots, for garnish

SERVES 6
as an appetizer

1 In a large saucepan, boil the sweet potato in salted water over medium-high heat until it is soft, about 10 minutes. Then pour off all of the water. Set the pan over the hot burner and shake a few times to evaporate any excess water. Add ¼ cup of the heavy cream and 2 tablespoons of the butter to the sweet potato and with a potato masher, mash together until quite smooth. Season with salt, cover, and set aside.

2 Heat a large skillet over medium-high heat. Season the scallops and mushrooms with salt and pepper. Add the remaining 2 tablespoons butter and the rosemary sprig to the hot skillet and when the butter melts, add the scallops and mushrooms. Brown both sides of the scallops without cooking them all the way through. Most people prefer scallops if cooked to medium-rare. This will take only a couple minutes on each side. Give the mushrooms the same treatment. With a slotted spoon, transfer the scallops to a large warm plate as they are done. Continue to cook the mushrooms for about 5 minutes longer. Add the mushrooms to the plate with the scallops.

3 The butter left in the skillet should now be nice and brown, but not burnt. Discard the rosemary sprig. Deglaze the pan with the sherry and bring it up to a simmer over a low heat. Add the remaining 2 tablespoons of heavy cream and reduce the liquid by half. Season to taste with salt and pepper.

4 Meanwhile, reheat the mashed sweet potatoes. Plate the scallops in their shells on top of the mashed sweet potatoes and the mushrooms. Garnish with the pea shoots and serve.

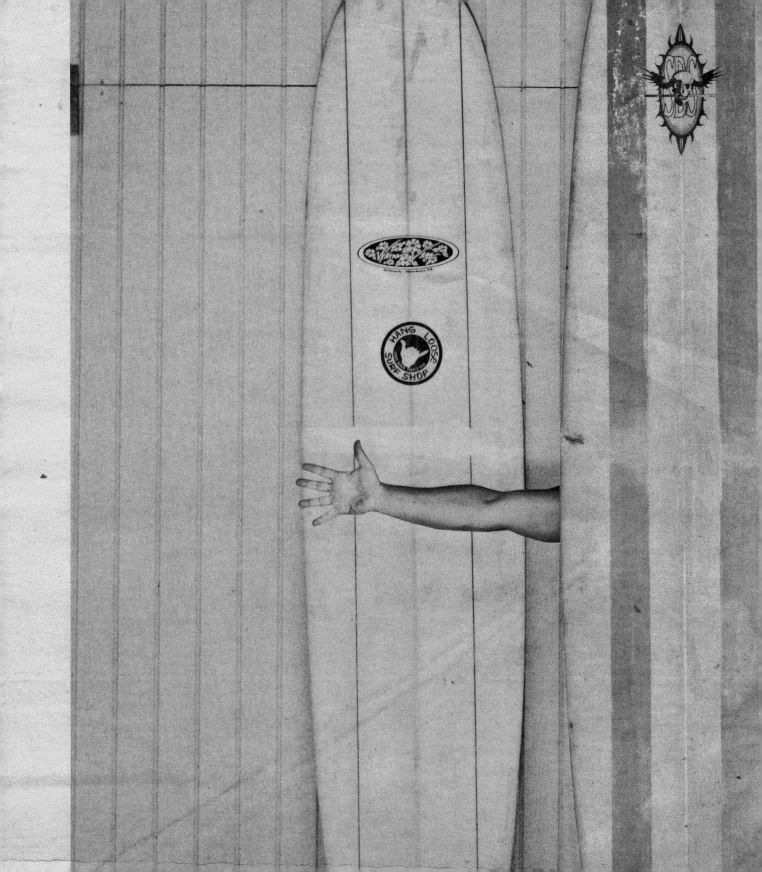

SEA URCHINS

I have scuba dived for urchins commercially. It looks easy, but actually, it is quite difficult. Prying them off a rock without breaking their delicate shells requires skill. They are mean little buggers, or at least well protected with prickly shells. However, inside the fierce armored urchin you will find soft, creamy roe sacs, which are one of the most highly prized seafood delicacies. These are actually the gonads. They have a slight iodine taste that gourmet chefs find desirable because its sharpness cuts through rich sauces, readying your palate for another bite.

Look for sea urchins in high-end fish markets and in Japanese markets. There are usually two different varieties, one from Santa Barbara and the other from Japan. From time to time you may also come across Maine urchins. The Santa Barbara urchin, a beautiful yellow color and very creamy, is the most popular (and costs more). The Japanese urchin, called *bufun*, is a darker yellow and has a mild flavor (and is cheaper). The Maine urchin has a more assertive taste. Whatever variety you use, remember that the roe is extremely delicate, so the best way to prepare it is raw or very lightly cooked. Also, check the sustainability before buying as regions change.

SEA URCHIN MISO SOUP
WITH CLAMS & SESAME

Marcia Kiesel came up with this recipe when I was thinking about a soup for sea urchin. Combining white wine with miso paste and soy sauce is a total fusion idea. The best way I can describe the effect of sea urchin here is that it makes the seafood even seafoodier. If you can get whole live sea urchins, use the shells as bowls and leave a few spines on them to wow, or at least wake up, your friends!

1 tablespoon sesame seeds

Salt

1 tablespoon vegetable oil

4 scallions, cut into 1-inch lengths

2 teaspoons minced peeled fresh ginger

¼ cup plus 2 tablespoons white wine

1 tablespoon blond miso paste

½ cup clam juice

2 teaspoons soy sauce

1 dozen littleneck clams or 3 dozen cockles, scrubbed

16 large sea urchin roe sacs

Japanese sesame oil, for serving

SERVES 4

1 In a medium saucepan, toast the sesame seeds over medium heat until golden, about 1 minute. Transfer the sesame seeds to a mortar and let cool completely. Add a pinch of salt to the mortar and with the pestle, pound the sesame seeds to a coarse texture.

2 In the saucepan, heat the oil. Add the scallions and ginger and cook over medium heat until softened, about 2 minutes. Add the wine and whisk in the miso paste until smooth. Add 1¼ cups of water, the clam juice, and the soy sauce and bring to a simmer. Add the clams, cover, and cook, shaking the pan a few times, until the clams open, about 3 minutes. Discard any clams that do not open after 3 minutes.

3 Divide the soup and clams among 4 bowls. Add 4 sea urchin roe sacs to each soup. Sprinkle with the crushed sesame seeds, add a few small drops of sesame oil, and serve.

SEA URCHIN CROSTINI
WITH CAULIFLOWER PUREE

Sea urchin roe is like a creamy butter of the sea, so it naturally takes to being married with butter and cream. This combination of sea urchin roe sitting on creamy, buttery cauliflower puree is so smooth! Next time you are thinking of serving a novel appetizer, instead of having oysters or clams on the half shell, try sea urchin roe on toast. You will thank me.

1 cup cauliflower in 1-inch florets

3 tablespoons heavy cream

Salt and freshly ground black pepper

16 baguette slices, sliced ¼ inch thick, about 2½ inches wide

Soft salted butter, for spreading

32 (1-inch-long) sea urchin roe sacs

Radish or broccoli sprouts, for garnish

Lemon wedges, for garnish

SERVES 4

1 In a small saucepan of boiling water, cook the cauliflower florets until tender, about 4 minutes. Drain thoroughly and transfer to a blender. Add the heavy cream and puree. Season with salt and pepper and refrigerate until chilled, about 30 minutes.

2 Toast the baguette slices and spread with butter.

3 Place a rounded teaspoon of cauliflower puree on each toast. Arrange 2 sea urchin roe sacs over each toast. Sprinkle with salt and top with a few sprouts. Serve with lemon wedges.

Sea urchin is so rich and flavorful. The first time I had anything like this I was sure there was cream in there, but guess what? Not a drop!

Flying SEA URCHIN PASTA
WITH FISH ROE & CHIVES

If I had to recommend a starter dish for the sea urchin newbie, this would be it. A basic culinary principle is if you can serve something with pasta, it has a pretty good shot at being appreciated. Think of this as heart-healthy spaghetti carbonara. I've begun to see a dish like this in the most hip Italian restaurants in Brooklyn and Lower Manhattan in the past few years. In my mind, it is simple perfection. The *uni* (Japanese for urchin) breaks down and becomes something like heavy cream while some added flying fish roe provides little crunchy bubbles that are truly delightful. It's so rich and flavorful. The first time I had anything like this I was sure there was cream in there, but guess what? Not a drop!

Flying fish roe is available in many Asian markets, where it is known as *tobiko*. You can also substitute *masago* (smelt roe) or cod roe, but if there's no roe to be had, the *uni* on its own will work fine.

¼ pound sea urchin roe sacs

¼ cup olive oil

⅛ teaspoon cayenne pepper

Salt

½ pound spaghetti

2 tablespoons unsalted butter, at room temperature

1 tablespoon *tobiko* (flying fish roe) or *masago* (smelt roe)

2 tablespoons chopped fresh chives

1 chive flower, separated into blossoms (optional)

SERVES 4
as an appetizer

1   In a blender, combine the sea urchin roe, olive oil, and cayenne pepper and puree.

2   In a large pot of boiling, salted water, cook the spaghetti until al dente. Just before draining, measure out ½ cup of the cooking water. Drain the pasta and add it back to the pot. Add the butter and stir to thoroughly coat the spaghetti. Add the sea urchin puree and 3 tablespoons of the pasta cooking water and stir over medium heat, adding more pasta water by the tablespoon, using most of it, until the pasta is coated with a creamy sauce. Do not boil. Remove the pot from the heat and taste for salt.

3   Divide the pasta among 4 bowls, top with *tobiko* and chives plus chive blossoms, if using, and serve.

SHRIMP

As soon as I first tasted the sweet flavor of shrimp as a youngster, I went through a phase where boiled shrimp was all I wanted. I wouldn't eat anything else. So my mom had to choose between sending me to school without breakfast or sending me to school on a full belly of shrimp. How many moms do you know who would cook their son shrimp for breakfast? Instead of cereal, eggs, and toast, she served me the tails, heads, and shells of shrimp and I ate them with gusto.

Many fishermen have little appetite for seafood because they're around the taste and smell of it all day. At the end of the day, all they want is a nice hamburger. Shrimpers are different. They eat shrimp while catching the little critters! I saw this in Canada, near Vancouver, where fishermen would haul up nets or traps of spotted prawns and eat them raw and twitching, sucking the heads and eating the tail meat. In Louisiana, likewise, while on their boats, Gulf Coast fishermen would throw shrimp in a pot of boiling water, add Cajun spices, and stir the shrimp with their fingers. Neat trick. I skip the fingers in the boiling water part and do my stirring with a wooden spoon.

I'm a "tail" guy. I love to eat the tail of the shrimp, which I think may well be the best part of it. I always tend to use head-on shrimp and cook them in the shell. It's fun to peel them yourself, getting all the juice on your hand, licking your fingers. Sloppy, yes, but so good!

SHRIMP BISQUE
WITH BASIL, BRANDY & SHERRY

For most people, bisque usually means lobster bisque. As much as I love it, I find it can be a major project to deal with all those shells, not to mention the cleanup of a pile of messy lobster shells. Shrimp shells are different. They don't take up as much space. I never throw them away because they have almost as much flavor as the shrimp meat. Stash them in the freezer and make a stock with them for soup and sauces. They give you all the heartiness and deep flavor of a lobster bisque but are so much easier to deal with; and the cleanup is a breeze.

2 tablespoons vegetable oil

1¼ pounds large shrimp, shelled and deveined, shells reserved, shrimp halved lengthwise

1 shallot, thinly sliced

Salt and freshly ground black pepper

3 tablespoons tomato paste

¼ cup brandy

2 cups clam juice

1½ cups heavy cream

3 tablespoons olive oil

1 tablespoon unsalted butter

1 large onion, diced

4 garlic cloves, thinly sliced

¼ teaspoon cayenne pepper, plus more for serving

¼ cup dry sherry

¼ cup chopped fresh basil, plus small leaves cut into very thin strips for serving

1 tablespoon fresh lemon juice

SERVES 4 TO 6

1 In a large pot, heat the vegetable oil. Add the shrimp shells and cook over medium-high heat, stirring, until starting to brown, about 3 minutes. Add the shallot, season with salt and pepper, and stir for 1 minute. Add the tomato paste and stir until glazed, about 1 minute. Stir in the brandy and simmer for 1 minute. Add the clam juice and 1 cup of water and bring to a boil, stirring until smooth, then partially cover, and simmer over low heat for 5 minutes. Add the cream, cover, and simmer for 20 minutes. Strain, pressing on the shells to get all the stock. Rinse the pot and replace on the stove.

2 In the large pot, heat 2 tablespoons of the olive oil and melt in the butter. Add the onion, garlic, and a pinch of salt and black pepper. Cover and cook over low heat, stirring a few times, until the onion is very soft, about 8 minutes. Raise the heat to medium, add the cayenne, and stir well. Add the sherry and cook for 1 minute. Stir in the strained shrimp stock and simmer over low heat for about 5 minutes. Pass the bisque through a strainer, pressing on the solids. Return the bisque to the pot, stir in the chopped basil and lemon juice, and season with salt and pepper.

3 Meanwhile, in a large skillet, heat the remaining 1 tablespoon of olive oil. Add the shrimp and season with salt and pepper. Cook over medium heat, stirring, until the shrimp are curled and just cooked, about 2 minutes. Stir the shrimp into the bisque. Ladle the bisque into bowls, top each with a few strips of basil and a pinch of cayenne, and serve.

The bisque can be refrigerated overnight.

MOFONGO
WITH SHRIMP & PEPPERS

I spend a lot of time in Puerto Rico and have made my fair share of mofongos, which are dishes cooked with plantains. The trick to mofongo is to get your plantain crust tasting nice and buttery and garlicky before the stew ingredients go in. This is a version of a classic dish using mashed plantains (or yucca). I think of it as the chowder of the Caribbean.

3 tablespoons olive oil

5 garlic cloves, 1 minced, 4 thinly sliced

1 large red cubanelle pepper, cored, seeded, and cut into ½-inch dice

1 jalapeño, seeded and minced

1 pound medium shrimp, shelled and deveined, shells reserved if making shrimp stock (see page 101, step 1)

Salt and freshly ground black pepper

1 cup clam juice or shrimp stock

1 tablespoon chopped fresh flat-leaf parsley

¼ pound salt pork, cut into ¼-inch dice

Vegetable oil, for frying

4 large green plantains, peeled and sliced ½ inch thick

SERVES 4

1 In a large skillet, heat 2 tablespoons of the olive oil. Add the minced garlic and cook over medium heat until fragrant, about 30 seconds. Add the cubanelle and jalapeño and cook until tender, about 4 minutes. Add the shrimp, season with salt and pepper, and cook, turning, until just cooked, about 3 minutes. Add the clam juice and parsley and remove from the heat.

2 Preheat the oven to 325°F. In a large cast-iron or nonstick skillet, cook the salt pork over medium heat until crisp, about 7 minutes. With a slotted spoon, transfer the salt pork to paper towels to drain. Pour off the fat and add ½ inch of vegetable oil to the skillet. When hot, add half the plantains and fry over medium-high heat until golden and tender, about 2 minutes per side. Transfer the fried plantains to a baking dish and hold in the oven while you fry the remaining plantains. Add the remaining fried plantains to the baking dish in the oven while you fry the garlic.

3 In a small skillet, heat the remaining 1 tablespoon of olive oil and add the sliced garlic. Cook over medium heat until golden, about 1½ minutes. Remove the baking dish from the oven and add the garlic mixture to the plantains. With a potato or bean masher, coarsely mash the plantains. Stir in the reserved crisp salt pork and season with salt.

4 Form the mash into 8 balls and place in the warm baking dish. Reheat the shrimp, peppers, and broth over medium-high heat for about 1 minute, then pour over the mofongo. Divide among 4 bowls and serve right away.

I spend a lot of time in
Puerto Rico and have made
my fair share of mofongos,
which are dishes cooked
with plantains.

If you are of an artistic frame of mind
and take the time to carve the papaya
delicately, it's also mind-blowingly
pretty. But you don't have to carve
it if all you want is a nice-looking
and delicious dish.

PAPAYA, PLANTAINS & SHRIMP
WITH PORK

I love tropical fruit with seafood, both of which are well represented in a dish called *piños* in Puerto Rico. I fill papaya halves with layers of fried, honeyed plantains, spicy ground pork, and then shrimp. Roasted over coals, the stuffed papaya is sweet, savory, spicy, and crazy good.

2 tablespoons vegetable oil, plus more for frying

½ pound medium shrimp, shelled and deveined, shells reserved

Salt

¼ cup dry white wine

½ pound ground pork

1 medium tomato, finely diced

1 small onion, finely diced

1 large garlic clove, minced

½ red bell pepper, cored, seeded, and finely diced

1 teaspoon sweet paprika

½ teaspoon ground cumin

¼ teaspoon chile flakes

1 large very ripe sweet plantain, peeled and cut into ¼-inch-thick slices

Honey

2 ripe papayas, halved and seeded

2 tablespoons freshly grated Parmesan cheese

SERVES 4

1 In a small saucepan, heat ½ tablespoon of the oil. Add the reserved shrimp shells and a pinch of salt and cook over medium-high heat, stirring, until the shells are orange and starting to brown, about 2 minutes. Add the wine and bring to a boil. Add 1 cup of water and simmer over medium heat for 10 minutes, then strain. You should have ½ cup of stock.

2 In a large skillet, heat 1 tablespoon of the oil. Add the ground pork, season with salt, and cook over medium-high heat, stirring, until browned, about 5 minutes. With a slotted spoon, transfer the pork to a medium bowl. Add the tomato, onion, garlic, and bell pepper and cook over medium-low heat, stirring a few times, until soft, about 10 minutes. Return the pork to the skillet and stir in the paprika, cumin, and chile flakes and cook over medium-high heat until fragrant, about 1 minute. Add the shrimp stock and simmer for 2 minutes. Remove from the heat.

3 In a large nonstick skillet, heat ½ inch of oil until very hot. Working in 2 batches, fry the plantain slices over medium-high heat until richly browned, about 3 minutes per side. Drain on paper towels and place on a large plate. While still hot, brush both sides with honey and sprinkle with a little salt. Repeat with the remaining plantain slices.

4 Light a grill. Place each papaya half on a large piece of foil, cut side up. Place the plantain slices in the papayas. Fill them with the pork mixture. Toss the shrimp with the remaining ½ tablespoon of oil and season with salt. Arrange equal amounts of the shrimp on top of each papaya over the pork. Sprinkle with the Parmesan and wrap up the papayas in the foil. If using charcoal, push the hot coals to one side of the grill. If using a gas grill, turn off the two side burners, leaving the center one on medium-high heat. Place the papaya packages opposite the hot coals sideways, or on both sides of the center gas burner. Cover and cook until tender, turning the papayas around halfway through, about 30 minutes total cooking time. Serve hot.

The shrimp stock and pork filling can be refrigerated overnight. Bring to room temperature before using.

SQUID

I happen to love squid and it's cheap, plentiful, and sustainable, so go ahead and squid it up! I am glad to see squid has become more popular on small-plate bar menus in recent years. It's pretty much everywhere these days. When I was a kid, I didn't find squid on many menus apart from Italian seafood places, where they were always fried, often rubbery, and drowned in marinara sauce that was so good that the squid didn't really matter. It was something chewy that you put sauce on. If you treat them with tender loving care, squid are very nice and tender. Apparently big fish figured this out a long time ago because they devour squid with abandon. They have long been one of the most popular angling baits wherever they are in nature. The key to delicious squid, as in so much else with seafood, is don't overcook it! If I have some on hand I toss it into soups, stews, and chowders, whether the recipe calls for it or not. It always adds toothsome and flavorful fun.

I used to jig for these guys at night on the Vineyard as they would pack into Menemsha Harbor. We used spotlights off the docks to shine into the water and attract them. It was really exciting because squid are aggressive and they put on quite a show as they glow in the water and jet about in a crazed feeding frenzy. All the kids would gather around the docks vying for a good spot. The nature of the sport is to reel fast and jig hard. With every few turns of the reel, give a gigantic pull on the rod. That's where you need to be careful. The jig is either a small squid-like shape with a few rows of nasty spines facing forward or a three-pronged hooked affair with a weight in the middle. When you yank on any jig, it sometimes has a tendency to come flying out of the water, where it can connect in a bad way with the fisherman. Some of the bigger kids viewed squidding as a prelude to going farther out on the jetty to hook some huge stripers and bluefish. Back in those early squidding years I left the jetty-hopping to the big kids and was happy to return home with a pailful of fresh squid that my mom would cook up. If you don't jig for your own squid, look for frozen whole small squid from California. They are the sweetest and most tender.

Simple SQUID PAELLA

Squid ink is often used to color and flavor a dish, especially rice. Although I love rice bursting with squid-ink flavor, for this paella I feel that keeping the ink in reserve as its own special and separate flavor makes for an elegant, briny, slightly iodine touch that refreshes the palate. You can buy packets of squid ink at seafood markets. They keep almost indefinitely. As for the rice, Spanish tradition for paellas calls for Valencia or Bomba rice because those short grains swell to soft, flavorful plumpness. A good Italian risotto rice such as Arborio also fits the bill.

3 tablespoons olive oil

1 cup Valencia, Bomba, or Arborio rice

1 tablespoon tomato paste

1 garlic clove, minced

1 teaspoon smoked sweet paprika

⅛ teaspoon cayenne pepper

Pinch of saffron

½ cup dry white wine

1½ cups clam juice

¾ pound small squid, bodies 4 to 5 inches long, cut into thin rings, tentacles whole

Salt

Optional garnish mixture: 1 tablespoon olive oil, 1 tablespoon squid ink, and 2 teaspoons lemon juice; or lemon wedges

SERVES 4

1 In a 9- to 10-inch-wide, deep skillet, heat the olive oil. Add the rice and cook over medium-high heat, stirring, until it starts to toast, about 2 minutes. Add the tomato paste, garlic, paprika, cayenne, and saffron and cook, stirring, for 1 minute. Add the wine, clam juice, and 2½ cups water and boil over medium-high heat for 10 minutes, stirring once or twice.

2 Reduce the heat to low and simmer until the rice is almost tender, about 7 minutes longer. Stir once or twice if the rice starts to stick to the skillet. Stir in the squid, cover, and cook, stirring a few times, until the squid is tender, about 3 minutes longer. Season with salt and divide among 4 shallow bowls. To make the garnish, in a small bowl, combine the olive oil, squid ink, and lemon juice. Drizzle over the paella and serve. Or just serve with lemon wedges.

For you masochist gourmets, see Matt's recipe in the lobster section (Lobster & Smoked Chicken Paella, page 59).

SQUID in spicy STEW
WITH BLACK BEANS & ASPARAGUS

Instead of squid ink, this soup gets its color from Chinese black bean sauce, which has a pungent and funky flavor. The fresh spring vegetables make this a recipe that is powerfully flavored but light and delicate as well.

1 cup asparagus or sugar snap peas, cut crosswise into ½-inch pieces

1½ tablespoons vegetable oil

2 garlic cloves, minced

1 tablespoon minced peeled fresh ginger

¼ teaspoon chile flakes

¼ cup dry white wine

1½ tablespoons Chinese plain black bean sauce

1½ tablespoons Chinese oyster sauce

Pinch of sugar

1 pound small cleaned squid, bodies cut into ¼-inch rings, tentacles whole

Salt and freshly ground black pepper

2 tablespoons chopped fresh chives

Steamed rice or warm bread and butter, for serving

SERVES 4

1 In a small saucepan, bring 1 cup of water to a boil. Add the asparagus and boil until just tender, about 2 minutes. Strain the asparagus and reserve ½ cup of the cooking water.

2 In a large skillet, heat the oil. Add the garlic and ginger and cook over medium heat until fragrant, about 3 minutes. Add the chile flakes and cook, stirring, for 30 seconds. Add the wine and simmer for 1 minute. Whisk in the black bean and oyster sauces, the sugar, and the reserved asparagus water and bring to a simmer. Add all the squid pieces, cover, and simmer over medium-low heat, stirring a few times, until the squid is tender, about 2 minutes. Add the asparagus and season with salt and pepper.

3 Ladle the stew into bowls, garnish with the chives, and serve with rice or bread.

BABY SQUID SAUTÉ
WITH GREEN GARLIC SAUCE

Green garlic sauce, also known as salsa verde, has long been one of the mainstays of old-fashioned Spanish restaurants, the kind that would have neon signs of glowing lobsters and shrimp and that magic word *mariscos*. I was a grown man before I knew that it referred to shellfish. To me, it always conjured up an image of shrimp, clams, squid, and mussels smothered in an herbaceous, garlicky green sauce. I thought the green sauce made it mariscos. This is my version of green sauce shellfish. Baby squid are super-tender and cook very quickly, which makes them well suited to putting a quick char on them. I was amused to visit the television set of *Extreme Chef* and watch Terry French (a great chef, fisherman, and U.S. Navy vet) use the flame of a camping stove to put a char on his squid. He stuffed his squid with U.S. Army rations and, believe it or not, it tasted pretty good!

¼ cup olive oil, plus more for frying

6 garlic cloves, minced

2 shallots, minced

2 cups fresh cilantro leaves and small sprigs, finely chopped in a food processor, plus extra for garnish

¼ cup dry white wine

2 tablespoons fresh lemon juice

Salt and freshly ground black pepper

16 baby squid bodies (fresh or frozen)

16 baby squid tentacles (fresh or frozen)

4 cups steamed rice, for serving

SERVES 4

1 In a large lightweight skillet, heat the oil. Add the garlic and cook over medium heat until golden and fragrant, about 3 minutes. Add the shallots and cook over low heat until softened, about 3 minutes. Add the cilantro and stir well. Add the wine and simmer over medium heat for 1 minute. Add the lemon juice, season with salt and pepper, cover, and remove from the heat.

2 In a large heavy skillet, such as cast iron, heat a thin layer of olive oil until very hot. Pat the squid bodies and tentacles very dry with paper towels and add one quarter of the squid to the skillet so it's not crowded. Season with salt and pepper. Cook over high heat until seared and just cooked, about 1½ minutes per side. Don't stir the squid and release any juices; once the squid is added to the skillet, just let it sear. Transfer the seared squid to the skillet with the sauce. Repeat with the remaining squid.

3 Gently reheat the squid in the sauce, garnish with cilantro, and serve with rice.

FIN FISH

BLACK-FISH

Thank the Narragansett Indians from my home turf for the name *tautog*, which is what we always called blackfish. These fish live around pilings and in the shadows, hence their dark color. They are super-delicious. They aren't commercially fished that much, which means there are plenty left over for you and me. I like that they are usually way inshore, often in back bays and other calm water, so they are a great fish for a non-strenuous day in the boat with some kids or older anglers.

I was once fishing for blackfish in the East River with my buddy Denton, a West Indian guy with impressive dread-locks. Denton is a big personality on the North Sixth Street Pier in Williamsburg, Brooklyn, which is a major fishing scene. We went a little upstream to Greenpoint and Denton was fishing on a jetty that required a semi-legal hop down to the water's edge. This all depends on your point of view

on the meaning of NO TRESPASSING signs. Denton climbed down on the rocks and hooked a nice blackfish. As he was lifting the rod and pulling the fish out of the water, a big furry animal (a muskrat?) scooted out and grabbed the blackfish off the end of the line and pulled it down into its little hole in the rocks! This really spooked Denton. Not only was he left with an empty hook, he was also scared off his secret fishing spot for a bit. That is, until he showed up with an eleven-foot pole, so he could fish from the safety of the parking lot, extending the pole over the rocks to the edge of the water without hav-ing to climb through furry-animal territory.

As he was lifting the rod and pulling the fish out of the water, a big furry animal (a muskrat?) scooted out and grabbed the blackfish off the end of the line and pulled it down into its little hole in the rocks!

BLACKFISH CHOWDER

Usually when there are blackfish fillets at the fish market, there are whole fish on sale, too. It's a crime to completely ignore the whole fish. That's a major chowder opportunity since you can utilize the sweet flesh, the big head, and the great bones. You really can't cook the fillet with the skin on, though, because it's too leathery. Put the skin in the stock. If you don't want to make the stock from scratch, any fish stock or even clam juice will do just fine.

3 tablespoons olive oil

6 (¼-inch-thick) slices pancetta (about 6 ounces), cut into ¼-inch dice

1 tablespoon unsalted butter

1 large onion, chopped

2 celery stalks, finely diced

2 bay leaves

2 sprigs fresh thyme

2 pounds red-skinned potatoes, peeled and cut into 1-inch dice

2 quarts Fish Stock (opposite), made with blackfish, or clam juice

1 cup chopped fresh flat-leaf parsley

1 teaspoon finely grated lemon zest

2 scallions, minced

Salt and freshly ground black pepper

1 pound blackfish fillets, skinned and cut into 1-inch pieces

½ cup light cream

SERVES 6

1   In a large pot, heat 1 tablespoon of the olive oil. Add the pancetta and cook over medium heat, stirring a few times, until browned and crisp, about 7 minutes. With a slotted spoon, transfer the pancetta to paper towels to drain. Pour off all but 2 tablespoons of the fat in the pot.

2   Add the butter and when melted, add the onion, celery, bay leaves, and thyme sprigs and cook over medium heat, stirring a few times, until softened, about 7 minutes. Add the potatoes and stock and bring to a boil. Simmer over medium-low heat until the potatoes soften, about 20 minutes. With a fork, mash about half the potatoes against the side of the pot to thicken the chowder.

3   Meanwhile, finely chop the pancetta with the parsley and transfer to a small bowl. Stir in the lemon zest, scallions, and remaining 2 tablespoons olive oil. Season with pepper.

4   Season the blackfish pieces with salt and pepper, add to the chowder with the cream, and simmer over low heat until the fish is just cooked, 3 to 4 minutes. Remove from the heat, discard the bay leaves and thyme sprigs, and season with salt and pepper.

5   Ladle the chowder into bowls. Pass the pancetta gremolata to stir into the soup.

The soup and gremolata can be refrigerated, separately, for up to 2 days.

FISH STOCK

This simple stock can be made with any white-fleshed fish. It is a good foundation for sauces or stews, adds some flavor to soups and chowders, and is the perfect medium to add delicate flavor to poached fish. It also makes me feel moral because I get to use the head, skeleton, and even the skin of any fish I catch rather than just saving the fillets and discarding the rest of the fish.

2 tablespoons olive oil

3 to 3½ pounds fresh fish head and bones, rinsed

4 scallions, chopped

3 sprigs fresh thyme

4 sprigs fresh parsley

Salt and freshly ground black pepper

½ cup white wine

MAKES 2 QUARTS

1 In a large pot, heat the olive oil. Add the fish head and bones, scallions, thyme, and parsley and season with salt and pepper. Cook over medium heat until the fish head turns opaque on the bottom, about 2 minutes. Stir the bones and cook for a few minutes longer, until all the bones are opaque. Add the wine and cook for 1 minute. Add 2 quarts of water and bring to a simmer.

2 Simmer the stock over medium-low heat for 20 minutes, then strain the stock.

The stock can be refrigerated for up to 2 days or frozen for up to 2 months.

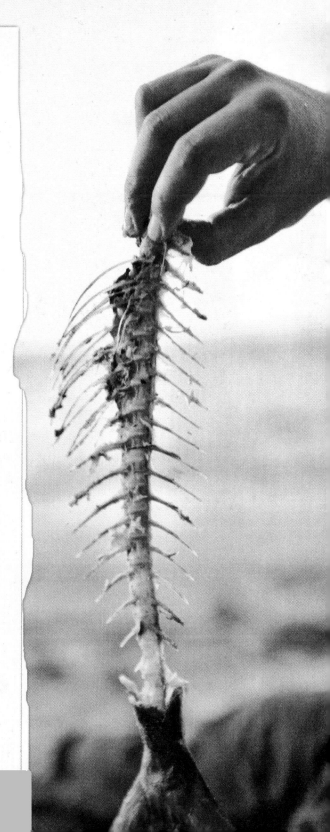

REDDENED BLACKFISH

Reddened blackfish is one of the great American recipe inventions of the past fifty years. It was the brainchild of "the amazin' Cajun" Paul Prudhomme from bayou country in the western part of Louisiana. Years later, another wonderful chef in Lafayette, Louisiana, came up with this variation using the blackening method in such a way that the fish turn red. I still get a kick out of the fact that there are recipes for reddened blackfish and blackened redfish.

1 tablespoon sweet paprika

1½ teaspoons hot paprika

½ teaspoon smoked sweet paprika

4 (8-ounce) blackfish fillets, skinned

Salt and white pepper

3 tablespoons vegetable oil

3 tablespoons fresh lemon juice

3 tablespoons unsalted butter

1 teaspoon harissa (optional)

Lemon wedges, for serving

SERVES 4

1. In a small bowl, combine the sweet, hot, and smoked sweet paprikas. Sprinkle the blackfish with the paprikas and season with salt and white pepper.

2. In a large nonstick skillet, heat the oil until shimmering. Add the blackfish and cook over medium-high heat until nicely glazed, about 3 minutes. Reduce the heat to medium and turn the blackfish. Cook about 4 minutes longer, until just cooked through and the fish starts to flake apart. Have a medium bowl near the stove and tilt the skillet, carefully pouring off most of the oil while using a spatula to hold the fish in place. Add the lemon juice, butter, and harissa, if using, to the skillet, and with a spoon, baste the blackfish with the glaze for about 10 seconds.

3. Place a blackfish fillet on each plate. Pour the glaze over and serve with lemon wedges.

BLUE-FISH

Blues, as bluefish are affectionately known, are among the most undervalued fish in the United States for both their fight and their flavor. I am, you should excuse the expression, a Masshole . . . as in a dude from Massachusetts who talks a lot about "the Sox and chowdah." Anyway, a Masshole grows up thinking it is a close contest between bluefish and striped bass for first place in the eating department. Many people are put off by the taste of bluefish, saying it really tastes "too fishy." I think what they are saying is that "it's very oily," and I have learned that all oily fish have to be prepared absolutely fresh before the oil reacts with the air. But that same high oil content makes bluefish a great fish to grill, smoke, and even add to chowdah. Get fresh bluefish on a plate in under twenty-four hours and your opinion of it will be changed forever.

Now, as a surfer, I have a different feeling about blues. I respect them and give them room. I have been bitten by blues (mostly the nasty little guys we call snappers) more times than I can count. It's a scary fish when you are surfing and a school of them are in a feeding frenzy smashing the underside of your board and churning up the surface into a whitewash! Also, they are determined little buggers. They don't let go once they have your finger. My best method for avoiding this situation when I see blues headed my way is to paddle like a maniac, giving the blues the right of way; or, if I can't get out of their way, I lift my feet onto the long board. Use pliers when taking a hook out of their mouth or you will learn about their teeth the hard way. I promise!

You'll notice all my bluefish recipes call for fresh-caught bluefish. More than with most other fish, buying bluefish is a crapshoot. You don't want to give the fish oil a chance to oxidize. Ask your fishmonger if the fish has been bled and see if the gills are cut free or pulled out (which is preferable).

CAPE COD BLUEFISH CHOWDER

I made this chowder on Cape Cod when my buddy Jamie had taken me to meet this group of communal livers—or maybe lovers—who work and live on a beautiful piece of land. They had really superb potatoes and were all for bartering a bed for a chowder, which seemed fair to me. I made this chowder as my part of the deal. Not only did everyone go bonkers for the chowder, but once they started to sniff the aromas wafting out of the barn where the kitchen was, new people materialized out of the woods with children in tow and bearing gifts in exchange for a bowl of chowder. It was such a big hit that the commune offered me a room for the summer. I didn't take them up on it, even though that barn was as near to great fishing and surfing as one could hope for. Guess I'm not the commune type.

½ pound thickly sliced bacon, cut into 1-inch pieces

2 tablespoons unsalted butter

1 large sweet onion, cut into ½-inch dice

1 fennel bulb, trimmed, cored, and cut into ½-inch dice, all fronds chopped

1 red or yellow bell pepper, cored, seeded, and cut into ½-inch dice

2 fresh thyme sprigs, plus 1 teaspoon chopped fresh thyme

1 bay leaf

Salt and freshly ground black pepper

1 pound medium red-skinned potatoes, halved, then quartered

1½ teaspoons sweet paprika

1 teaspoon hot paprika

1 teaspoon dry mustard

1 cup chopped canned tomatoes, preferably fire-roasted

2 cups Fish Stock (page 113) or clam juice

5 ounces cleaned spinach or 1 cup frozen leaves, thawed

1½ pounds skinned and trimmed bluefish fillet, red oil line cut out, in 1 or 2 pieces

2 tablespoons chopped fresh dill or flat-leaf parsley

SERVES 6

1. In a large pot, cook the bacon over medium heat until crisp but not too dark, about 6 minutes. Drain the bacon on paper towels and keep about 1 tablespoon of the fat in the pot, pouring off the rest. Add the butter to the pot and melt. Then add the onion, fennel, bell pepper, thyme sprigs, and bay leaf, and season with salt and pepper. Cover and cook, stirring a few times, until soft, about 10 minutes. Add the potatoes and a pinch of salt, cover, and cook until the potatoes start to stick to the pot and brown, about 3 minutes. Stir in the sweet and hot paprikas and mustard and cook for about 1 minute, until fragrant. Stir in the tomatoes and stock and raise the heat to medium-high. Stir to scrape up the flavors stuck on the bottom of the pot, then add 1 cup of water and bring to a simmer.

2. Add half the cooked bacon to the pot, reserving the rest for serving. Simmer the chowder over low heat, partially covered, for about 10 minutes. Then check the potatoes and mash any tender ones against the side of the pot to help thicken the chowder. Partially cover and check a few times over the next 5 minutes as the potatoes cook.

3. Meanwhile, bring a medium saucepan with 1 inch of water to a boil. Add the spinach, stirring it in as it wilts, and cook for 1 minute. Drain, lightly squeeze out the water, and chop.

4. Season the bluefish with salt and pepper and place in the chowder, almost submerged. Cover and simmer over low heat until the fish is just cooked, 10 to 15 minutes. With a long spatula, lift the bluefish fillet out of the chowder and onto a large plate. Discard the thyme sprigs and bay leaf.

5. Add the spinach to the pot and simmer for a few minutes, until tender. Season with salt and pepper. Gently break up the bluefish and fold into the chowder along with the dill and chopped thyme. Serve in bowls with crisp bacon on top.

Hot SMOKED BLUEFISH

This might be the best thing in the entire world. Don't be scared to try hot smoking. It's really, really easy. Think of it as regular grilling with a little added flavor. I don't see how one can mess this up—and trust me, I can mess up! So long as the wood chips are wet and soaked through, you can put them anywhere on the grill and still get awesome flavor. Go for it. All you need is a simple hibachi or a small Weber or other brand of covered grill. I have often used a little steel box filled with chips for smokiness. A small box fashioned from aluminum foil works fine, too. This is great served warm with any cooking juices over steamed rice, mixed with grilled corn, or served chilled with potato salad. And leftovers make for a great Smoked Bluefish Dip (page 122).

2 tablespoons soy sauce

1 tablespoon Dijon mustard

1 teaspoon sugar

2 bluefish fillets (1½ pounds total), skinned, red oil line cut out

2 teaspoons coarsely cracked black pepper

2 cups hardwood chips, soaked in water for 30 minutes

3 to 4 cups steamed rice, for serving (optional)

SERVES 4

1 In a large shallow dish, combine the soy sauce, mustard, and sugar. Add the bluefish fillets and coat with the marinade. Refrigerate for 2 to 3 hours.

2 Light a charcoal fire and push the coals to one side of the grill. Put the bluefish fillets skinned side down on a double layer of heavy-duty foil, folding up the edges around the fish slightly. Do not enclose. Sprinkle the pepper over the top. Place the fish to the edge of the hot coals. Drain the wood chips and scatter half over the hot coals. Cover and cook, turning the fish around once, halfway through, for about 20 minutes, until the fish is just cooked. Add the remaining chips halfway through cooking.

3 Remove the fish from the foil, and let cool to warm. Serve warm and pour the cooking juices over the fish and rice, if serving.

The smoked bluefish can be refrigerated for up to 4 days.

And leftovers make for a great Smoked Bluefish Dip (page 122).

SMOKED BLUEFISH DIP

I'm guessing this is one of the recipes handed down by the gods because it's insanely delicious and seems to have been here from the beginning of time. I have certainly eaten it my whole life. It's an old standby and I wouldn't consider any book of mine complete without it. When I serve this appetizer to guests, it is eaten up really fast; and quite often, everyone is then too stuffed for dinner. Cool thing about this is that you can use the leftovers from the Hot Smoked Bluefish (page 120). Serve with vegetables or crackers.

½ pound Hot Smoked Bluefish (page 120), chilled

¼ cup mayonnaise

¼ cup sour cream

1 medium shallot, minced

2 tablespoons chopped fresh dill

2 tablespoons capers, drained and chopped

2 tablespoons fresh lime juice

Paprika, for serving

MAKES ABOUT
1½ CUPS
4 to 6 servings

1   Flake the smoked bluefish into a medium bowl. Stir in the mayonnaise, sour cream, shallot, dill, capers, and lime juice. Refrigerate until chilled and firm.

2   Stir well. Sprinkle with paprika and serve.

The dip can be refrigerated for up to 3 days.

My advice is to put out only a little dip on the table if you want your friends to eat dinner, too. No joke.

WHOLE BLUEFISH in FOIL

Don't worry about coating the fish with lots of mayonnaise—you will not taste it, but it will keep the fish moist during baking and incredibly tasty.

4-pound whole bluefish, gutted and scaled

Salt and freshly ground black pepper

¼ cup mayonnaise

2 lemons, thinly sliced

10 sprigs fresh flat-leaf parsley

1 medium onion, thinly sliced

½ red bell pepper, cored, seeded, and thinly sliced

½ yellow bell pepper, cored, seeded, and thinly sliced

½ orange bell pepper, cored, seeded, and thinly sliced

2 cups cherry tomatoes

Sweet paprika, for dusting

SERVES 4 TO 6

1   Preheat the oven to 500°F. Rinse the bluefish and pat dry with paper towels. Select a rimmed baking sheet large enough to hold the fish (the fish can be set on the diagonal across the sheet). Tear off 2 large sheets of heavy-duty foil, making sure the foil overlaps the pan by about 6 inches on both sides. Overlap the foil strips on the pan so there are no bare spots. Place the bluefish in the center of the foil-lined sheet. Season inside and out with salt and pepper. Spread the mayonnaise in the cavity and all over the outside of the fish. Arrange half of the lemon slices and all of the parsley sprigs in the cavity of the bluefish and the remaining lemon slices on top. Arrange the onion, followed by the red bell pepper, yellow bell pepper, and orange bell pepper slices over and around the top of the fish. Add the cherry tomatoes and dust the top of the fish with the paprika. Place 2 more sheets of foil over the fish, folding up the edges to enclose the fish.

2   Reduce the oven temperature to 400°F. Put the fish in the oven and bake for about 40 minutes, until the fish flakes at the thickest part, past the head to the shoulder area. An instant-read thermometer should register 120°F to 125°F. Remove from the oven and let the fish rest in the foil for about 5 minutes. **To grill the whole bluefish:** Place the foil-wrapped fish over a medium-hot fire, cover, and cook, rotating the package a few times for even cooking over 20 minutes, until you hear the juices simmering and the package expands. Remove the package from the grill and let rest for 3 to 4 minutes.

3   Open the foil. With 2 forks, scrape off the skin and dark oil line. Lift the meat from the bluefish and place it on a large plate or platter. Lift the bones to get at the meat on the other side of the bluefish and place that on the platter. Pour the vegetables and any juices over the bluefish and serve.

CARP

Carp are not a native fish, but they sure have taken well to American waters. I find them everywhere. Technically speaking, they are large goldfish. In terms of angling, though, they fight like sharks. In recent years, flyfishermen (who can tend to get snooty about fishing for "coarse fish"—i.e., not salmon or trout) have discovered that they are really good sporting fish. On a slow day on the Missouri, when the trophy trout have decided to take the day off, a fifteen-pound carp at the end of your line can brighten your mood.

The first carp I ever caught was in Kissena Lake, a freshwater pond in Queens. That fish scared the hell out of me. It hit like a freight train and pulled line off my reel for ten minutes. My Polish buddies from Greenpoint, there on the waterfront in Queens, were shocked to learn I had thrown back my catch, which is something they rarely do. Truth is, I lost the fish at my feet! The city says it's illegal to take them, and that makes no sense to me, because they are illegal to put in there in the first place! Basically we are talking about two species, the common carp and the Asian carp. Both are used in cooking, but my personal experience has only been with common carp.

The Poles, in fact all Central Europeans, have wonderful ways of making carp. They say it's especially good when it comes out of cold waters, which is probably one of the reasons that the Jewish delicacy gefilte fish is such a favorite at Passover (which falls around Easter, before the water has warmed too much). In some cultures, it is considered a great honor to be served the head of a carp.

CARP CHOWDER
WITH SAUERKRAUT & PAPRIKA

Carp is especially good when gently poached. Instead of trying to remove pin bones from the fillets, poach it first, and then the bones come right out. Big, thick carp fillets take very well to traditional European flavors such as paprika, sauerkraut, and dill. The fillets simmer in the soup and are then lifted out whole to debone. The fish can then be broken up and added back into the soup.

2 tablespoons unsalted butter

1 medium onion, finely chopped

1 garlic clove, minced

1½ teaspoons sweet paprika

1 teaspoon hot paprika, plus more for sprinkling

1 (14.5-ounce) can Italian-style stewed tomatoes, chopped, juices reserved

2 cups clam juice

1 pound red potatoes, peeled and cut into 1-inch dice

1 pound skinned carp fillet

½ cup sauerkraut

Salt and freshly ground black pepper

3 tablespoons chopped fresh dill

Sour cream, for serving

SERVES 4 TO 6

1 In a large pot, melt the butter. Add the onion and garlic and cook over medium heat until softened, about 7 minutes. Add the sweet and hot paprikas and cook, stirring, for 1 minute. Add the tomatoes and juices, the clam juice, ½ cup of water, and the potatoes, and bring to a simmer. Cook, partially covered, until the potatoes are soft, about 20 minutes. With a fork, crush some of the potatoes against the side of the pot to thicken the chowder.

2 Add the carp fillet and simmer over low heat until just cooked, about 7 minutes. With a spatula, carefully lift the carp from the chowder and onto a large plate. Pull the bones from the fillet, break up the carp into bite-size pieces, and add it back to the chowder. Add the sauerkraut and simmer for 1 or 2 minutes to heat through. Season with salt and pepper and add the dill.

3 Ladle the chowder into mugs or bowls, sprinkle each with hot paprika, and pass the sour cream at the table.

ZINFANDEL CARP

This recipe is a take on a traditional Eastern European method of poaching freshwater fish wherein a bit of honey is used for sweetness and complexity. The thick fillets are meaty. White wine sauces are often made for carp, but a red wine sauce is more intense and savory. Especially if made, as I made it here, with a "chewy" Zinfandel.

Wine sauce

8½ tablespoons unsalted butter, cut into tablespoons and chilled

1 medium shallot, minced

¾ cup Zinfandel

1 teaspoon honey

1½ teaspoons chopped fresh thyme

Salt and freshly ground black pepper

Poached carp

¼ cup Zinfandel

4 thin lemon slices

2 bay leaves

Salt and freshly ground black pepper

4 (8-ounce) carp fillets, skinned

SERVES 4

1 To make the wine sauce: In a medium skillet, melt ½ tablespoon of the butter. Add the shallot and cook over low heat until softened, about 4 minutes. Add the wine and boil over medium-high heat until reduced to ¼ cup, about 8 minutes. Reduce the heat to low and, using a small whisk, add 1 tablespoon of the butter, swirling it in until blended. It should not simmer, but should remain very warm to hold the emulsion. Remove the skillet from the heat if the sauce gets too hot. Keep adding the butter, 1 tablespoon at a time, carefully keeping the sauce from simmering, taking it on and off the heat. When all the butter has been incorporated and the sauce is smooth, off the heat, stir in the honey and thyme and season with salt and pepper. Set aside.

2 To prepare the carp: In a large, deep skillet, combine 1 quart of water, the wine, lemon slices, and bay leaves. Add 1 teaspoon of salt and bring to a boil. Cover and simmer over low heat for 5 minutes. Season the carp with salt and pepper and add to the simmering liquid. Simmer very gently over low heat until the carp is just done and starts to flake with a fork, 8 to 10 minutes.

3 Meanwhile, just before the fish is done, gently reheat the sauce over medium heat, whisking constantly and taking on and off the heat as needed to rewarm. With a slotted spoon, lift the carp from the cooking liquid onto a large plate and pat dry with paper towels. Place a carp fillet on each plate, spoon the sauce over, and serve.

Poets' POLISH CARP

3 tablespoons unsalted butter

3 tablespoons all-purpose flour, plus more for dredging fish

2 cups Freshwater Fish Stock (recipe follows)

1 cup dry red wine

¼ cup sliced almonds

¼ cup raisins

2 tablespoons honey

Kosher salt and freshly ground black pepper

1 teaspoon ground ginger

Juice of ½ lemon, plus lemon wedges for garnish

1 (3- to 4-pound) common carp, gutted and scaled, cut crosswise into 1-inch-thick steaks, head and tail removed and reserved for stock

3 tablespoons canola oil

Fresh flat-leaf parsley sprigs, for garnish

SERVES 4 TO 6

Kryz Drzewiecki has a restaurant—one of my main go-to places—named Krolewskie Jadlo, and it's just around the corner from me in Brooklyn. Before the hipsters and the supermodels moved in, my 'hood was super-Polish and I loved it! Kryz (Chris) has hung in there even as the espresso cafes and tapas bars and art galleries and boutique shops have taken over. This is a recipe he got from his mom that she makes at Christmastime, but Kryz isn't a stickler for the calendar. He cooks what he likes when he feels like it. Kryz gave me the assignment of cutting the carp into steaks. I thought this would be an easy job, but cutting through the backbone of a big carp takes linebacker biceps. Thank you, Kryz (and Mama Kryz), for letting me use this recipe in my first cookbook.

1 Melt the butter in a medium saucepan over medium heat. Whisk in the flour to incorporate and cook until smooth, 2 to 3 minutes. Whisk in the fish stock and red wine until incorporated, then stir in the almonds, raisins, and honey. Cook over low heat, stirring occasionally, until the sauce has thickened and the flavors have married, about 15 minutes. Season with salt and pepper and stir in the ginger and lemon juice. Keep warm.

2 Meanwhile, sprinkle the carp steaks with salt and pepper and dredge in flour to coat. Heat the oil in a nonstick sauté pan over medium-high heat until almost smoking. Cook the steaks until golden brown, 5 to 6 minutes (depending on the thickness of the steak). Flip the fish and continue to cook until the opposite side is golden brown, 4 to 5 minutes longer. Transfer the fish to plates and spoon a little sauce over the top. Garnish with lemon wedges and sprigs of parsley and serve immediately.

FRESHWATER FISH STOCK

Carp head and tail

5 or 6 allspice berries

5 or 6 dried bay leaves

2 celery stalks, roughly chopped

1 carrot, roughly chopped

1 yellow onion, roughly chopped

Place the carp head and tail in a large stockpot, followed by the allspice, bay leaves, celery, carrot, and onion. Cover completely with at least 6 cups of water and bring to a boil over medium-high heat. Reduce the stock to a simmer and cook, skimming scum off the top occasionally, for 1 hour. Strain the stock and discard the solids.

MAKES 4 CUPS

CAT-FISH

The first catfish I ever caught was in Florida. It was nighttime, and I was at the end of the dock, alone, on the edge of the mangroves. I dropped a line and when the fish took the bait, I was scared half to death; I hadn't expected to catch much that night, never mind a huge catfish. Once the fear turned into adrenaline and excitement, I got the better of the big catfish. I ran into the house where I was staying and showed off my impressive and unexpected catch, only to attract a flock of hungry pelicans. . . .

I've harvested farmed catfish, trapped wild ones, and even noodled for them. Noodling is a catfish-catching method that requires you to stick your hand into the lair of a catfish and hope that the fish latches on to your arm. The theory is that the fish is trying to protect its home and eggs. I did manage to noodle a fish, but the lady I was competing against in a noodling contest in Oklahoma whupped me something fierce.

I once ran a trapline for catfish with the mayor of Breaux Bridge, Louisiana, the crawfish capital of the world. Apart from his mayoral duties, he and his wife produce handmade catfish traps and they fish together whenever he is not mayor-

ing. It looked to me like they had set thousands of traps all throughout their area. They also sold their catch. Many states allow fishermen and -women to maintain registered cleaning facilities in back of their houses. You can actually skin, fillet, and sell wild catfish right from your home. Catfish are farmed extensively, which means they are a fairly sustainable fishery—and I always applaud that.

133

CATFISH STEW
WITH LIMA BEANS

Catfish is meaty and robust enough to stand up to the powerful flavors in this succotash-like stew. In Cajun country, it seems that everyone has a hunting and fishing camp and an old black iron pot that has cooked up a century's worth of meals. The combination of salt pork, cayenne, and tomatoes is the foundation of many fish stews. Light in body but deep in flavor, this is the kind of dish that warms your insides after a morning of duck hunting in your camp on the bayou.

2 tablespoons vegetable oil

2 (¼-inch-thick) slices salt pork, about 3 inches long

1 large onion, chopped

2 garlic cloves, minced

4 scallions, chopped

¼ to ½ teaspoon cayenne pepper

¼ cup tomato paste

2 cups tomato sauce

2 cups Fish Stock (page 113) or chicken stock

2 tablespoons Worcestershire sauce

Dried oregano, to season soup and fish

2 large fresh sage leaves

2 cups baby lima beans, fresh or frozen, or shell beans such as cowpeas or black-eyed peas

2 pounds skinned catfish fillets, cut into 1½-inch pieces

Salt and freshly ground black pepper

SERVES 4 TO 6

1 In a large heavy pot, heat the oil. Add the salt pork and cook over medium heat until browned, about 3 minutes per side. Add the onion and garlic and cook, stirring a few times, until very soft, about 8 minutes. Add the scallions and cayenne and cook for 1 minute. Add the tomato paste and cook, stirring, until glazed, about 1 minute. Stir in the tomato sauce, stock, Worcestershire, pinch of oregano, the sage leaves, and the lima beans and bring to a simmer. Cover and simmer over low heat until the flavors cook in and the limas are tender, about 30 minutes.

2 Season the catfish pieces with salt and pepper and oregano. Refrigerate for 5 to 10 minutes. Add the catfish to the stew, cover, and simmer on low until the catfish is tender, 15 to 20 minutes. Remove the salt pork and sage leaves and serve.

The stew can be refrigerated overnight and reheated.

Light in body but deep in flavor, this is the kind of dish that warms your insides after a morning of duck hunting in your camp on the bayou.

CATFISH SANDWICH
WITH DILL RÉMOULADE & SLICED JALAPEÑOS

Imagine yourself in a funky tavern run by some good ol' boys (and good ol' girls) from the Deep South, with timeworn plank floors and country music playing on the jukebox. Well, what you have imagined is Enid's, my local pub in Greenpoint, Brooklyn! These sons and daughters of Dixie know their catfish and have come up with one of the world's great sandwiches. The rémoulade rounds out the flavor of the crisp, salty fish and the jalapeños work their spicy magic to elevate the whole experience from merely great to Dixie-flavored divinity.

1 cup mayonnaise

½ cup chopped fresh dill

Juice of 1 lime

½ habanero chile, seeded and minced

1 cup all-purpose flour, plus more for dredging

1 teaspoon salt

1 teaspoon baking powder

1 (12-ounce) can of beer, plus more as needed

Vegetable oil, for frying

2 tablespoons Jamaican jerk paste, such as Busha Browne or Walkerswood

4 (½-pound) catfish fillets

4 large good-quality hamburger buns

Paper-thin slices of jalapeño

SERVES 4

1 In a small bowl, combine the mayonnaise, dill, lime juice, and habanero to make a rémoulade sauce. Keep the sauce in the refrigerator.

2 To make the batter, in a large bowl, combine the 1 cup of flour, salt, and baking powder. Lightly stir in the beer until the mixture is like pancake batter. Set aside for 30 minutes. Just before using, check the thickness of the batter; it may have thickened more after sitting. Lightly stir in a little more beer as needed.

3 In a large saucepan, heat 2 inches of oil to 350°F. Have a rack set over a rimmed baking sheet near the stove. Spread the jerk paste on the catfish fillets. Put some flour in a shallow dish. Working 2 at a time, dredge the catfish fillets in flour, shaking off excess. Dip in the batter, letting excess drip off. Fry, turning once, until browned and crisp, about 3 minutes. Transfer to the rack and repeat with the last catfish fillets.

4 Spread the dill rémoulade sauce on the bottom of each bun, add the fish, and top with more sauce and a few slices of jalapeño. Add the top of each bun and eat!

CATFISH KEBABS
WITH SPICY KETCHUP GLAZE

I invented this recipe for a family in Oklahoma who hosted me when I entered a noodling contest against a local legend. Despite my resounding defeat, I reclaimed some respect with this super-flavorful recipe.

½ cup ketchup or chili sauce

2 tablespoons soy sauce

2 tablespoons, packed, dark brown sugar

2 teaspoons habanero hot sauce

2 teaspoons chopped fresh rosemary

Salt and freshly ground black pepper

2 pounds catfish fillets, skinned and cut into 1½-inch chunks

16 slices narrow baguette, about ½ inch thick and
1 inch wide

Olive oil, for brushing

24 cherry tomatoes

8 slices bacon

SERVES 4

1 In a large bowl, combine the ketchup, soy sauce, brown sugar, hot sauce, and rosemary. Season lightly with salt and pepper and add the catfish chunks. Stir well to coat the catfish completely, cover, and refrigerate for a few hours or overnight.

2 Light a grill. Soak eight 8-inch bamboo skewers in water for 20 minutes, then drain. Brush the baguette slices on both sides with olive oil. Thread the ingredients onto the skewers, evenly spaced about a ½-inch apart. Thread the catfish, baguette slices, and tomatoes alternately. Loop in the bacon between the other ingredients.

3 Grill the kebabs over a medium-low fire, turning a few times, until nicely charred and the catfish flakes easily, 10 to 12 minutes. Transfer to plates and serve right away.

FLOUNDER

I've fished for flounder my whole life. As a kid I used an old-fashioned hand line. I loved fishing this way and kind of miss it. In my little Irish fishing sweater and holding a hand line I must not have looked much different from the kids on Cape Cod one hundred years ago. Fishing for flounder with sea worms from my grandpa's shop, I waited for the tap-tap on the line as the flounder nudged the bait. It felt really good. It seemed back then we always caught a lot.

Using that simple hand line, I'd haul in twenty flounder, all on my own! Then I'd take 'em to Pup, who would fillet the fish like a charter guy—just rip it apart—wasting little meat, and he was so fast! As a cook or chef you learn to fillet the proper way, which leaves no meat on the skeleton. But the real fishermen often don't have time for restaurant methods. Their version is fast and very impressive! We'd cook with cornmeal and butter. There's nothing better in the world than Pup's flounder. It tasted so amazing that I didn't realize that

catching twenty flounder at a time had a big impact on the number of flounder in the bay. Nobody told me my twenty trophies were affecting the bay's sustainability. We thought the flounder would be there forever, but overfishing has had its effect. Lesson learned.

Of all the fish in this book, I have found that flounder is the easiest sell, even to those who are not overly fond of fish. Its soft texture and super-mild taste are so pleasing and it has the ability to take on the flavor of whatever you cook it in. For people who claim they don't like fish, flounder usually works as the "gateway" fish.

FLOUNDER in GRAPE LEAVES

Cooking delicate fillets in grape leaves is insanely easy and kinda impressive. You simply wrap up the fillets in the leaves, along with some seasonings, and throw them on the grill until the leaves start to burn. At that point your fish is done, you have a dramatic package, and you open it to a blast of flavorful steam. I'm sold and you will be, too.

4 medium tomatoes or tomatillos

2 small garlic cloves, minced

1 tablespoon plus 1 teaspoon capers, drained and chopped

¼ cup olive oil, plus more for the grape leaves

Salt and freshly ground black pepper

4 (6- to 8-ounce) flounder fillets

8 to 12 large grape or fig leaves, stems removed

SERVES 4

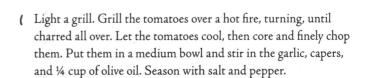

1 Light a grill. Grill the tomatoes over a hot fire, turning, until charred all over. Let the tomatoes cool, then core and finely chop them. Put them in a medium bowl and stir in the garlic, capers, and ¼ cup of olive oil. Season with salt and pepper.

2 Season the flounder with salt and pepper. Spread the tomato mixture over the fillets and wrap each one in 2 large leaves, enclosing the tomato mixture. Rub the leaves generously with olive oil. Grill the flounder over a medium-hot fire until the leaves are crisp and the flounder just cooked, about 3 minutes on the first side and 2 minutes on the second side. Serve right away.

Fig leaves will work just as well as grape leaves, but grape leaves can be found in the wild. Of course, if you don't feel like going grape-leaf picking, you can often find them in Middle Eastern or Greek markets.

Roasted WHOLE FLOUNDER
WITH TOMATO, HERBS & BUTTERED CROUTONS

Flounder is most often prepared from fillets, probably because they are so quick and easy to cook. But roasting a whole flounder isn't much trouble at all, and if you are the one doing the catching and cleaning, why not simplify your life? Flounder is very easy to roast whole, and then you can remove the fillet from the bones at the table. It also looks cool if you are good with a serving knife or spatula. A roasted whole fish somehow always seems to have more juiciness. This recipe calls for bread crumbs made from scratch, which is my preference, but to tell you the truth, store-bought bread crumbs work just fine.

2½ cups ½-inch crustless bread cubes, from 3 slices Tuscan or peasant bread

2 tablespoons olive oil

5 tablespoons unsalted butter, 3 tablespoons melted and reserved

1 cup ½-inch diced onion

16 cherry tomatoes, quartered

3 tablespoons chopped fresh basil

3 tablespoons minced fresh chives

Salt and freshly ground black pepper

3-pound whole flounder, or fluke, gutted and scaled (see Note, opposite, for removing fins and skinning)

¼ cup plus 2 tablespoons dry white wine

SERVES 3 TO 4

1 Preheat the oven to 350°F. Put the bread cubes on a rimmed baking sheet and drizzle with 1 tablespoon of the olive oil. Toss the bread to coat with the oil and spread in an even layer. Bake for about 10 minutes, until golden and crisp. Let cool. Increase the oven temperature to 450°F.

2 In a medium skillet, melt 2 tablespoons of the butter. Add the onion, cover, and cook over medium-low heat until softened, about 5 minutes. Add the tomatoes and cook, stirring a few times, until the tomatoes give off some juices, about 1 minute. With a rubber spatula, scrap the mixture into a large bowl. Add the bread cubes, basil, and chives, stir well, and season with salt and pepper.

3 Place the flounder on a rimmed baking sheet large enough to hold it (the fish can be set on the diagonal across the sheet). Rub the flounder, including the head and tail, with the remaining 1 tablespoon of oil. Put the flounder on the sheet with its white skin side down. Pour the wine over the fish and lift the fish to allow the wine to flow underneath, then rub wine over the top of the fish. Season the fish on both sides with salt and pepper. Drizzle the top of the fish with 2 tablespoons of the reserved melted butter, allowing the butter to run down the sides of the fish.

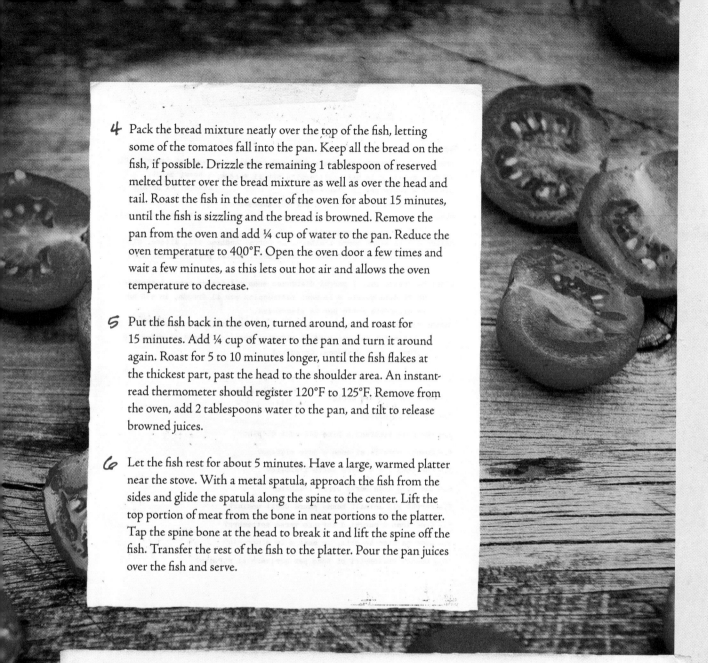

4 Pack the bread mixture neatly over the top of the fish, letting some of the tomatoes fall into the pan. Keep all the bread on the fish, if possible. Drizzle the remaining 1 tablespoon of reserved melted butter over the bread mixture as well as over the head and tail. Roast the fish in the center of the oven for about 15 minutes, until the fish is sizzling and the bread is browned. Remove the pan from the oven and add ¼ cup of water to the pan. Reduce the oven temperature to 400°F. Open the oven door a few times and wait a few minutes, as this lets out hot air and allows the oven temperature to decrease.

5 Put the fish back in the oven, turned around, and roast for 15 minutes. Add ¼ cup of water to the pan and turn it around again. Roast for 5 to 10 minutes longer, until the fish flakes at the thickest part, past the head to the shoulder area. An instant-read thermometer should register 120°F to 125°F. Remove from the oven, add 2 tablespoons water to the pan, and tilt to release browned juices.

6 Let the fish rest for about 5 minutes. Have a large, warmed platter near the stove. With a metal spatula, approach the fish from the sides and glide the spatula along the spine to the center. Lift the top portion of meat from the bone in neat portions to the platter. Tap the spine bone at the head to break it and lift the spine off the fish. Transfer the rest of the fish to the platter. Pour the pan juices over the fish and serve.

NOTE:

Set the flounder on a work surface with the dark skin side up. With sharp kitchen shears, cut around the flounder to remove the skirt of the fins neatly. With a boning knife, make an incision at the tail and cut under the skin, keeping the meat on the bone, to make a 1-inch or so tag to hold on to. Use a kitchen towel to grab the skin and start to pull up toward the head. If you see some of the meat is clinging to the skin, use the knife to cut under the skin and keep the meat down. Hold the tail and rip the skin from the fish. It should come off cleanly.

GROUPER

Groupers are big, hulking fish. Grouper fishing is popular all along the Gulf Coast and because it doesn't require a lot of finesse to hook one, the fish are very popular with anglers of all degrees of skill.

I rent a little getaway shack in a small fishing village in Puerto Rico where the commercial fishermen often have a grouper or two to sell. I must admit I am usually a customer because when I am spearfishing for grouper there I get so nervous that I'm going to misidentify one of the really endangered species of grouper, that I end up not shooting the speargun at all.

That sounds lame for a guy who is writing a book about the fish I catch and eat. But I'm just being honest here. You pay your money, you get your fish, real simple. But there is an art to finding a grouper at the right price. The transaction begins at the end of the day. Coming back from their work, the fishermen run their beautiful painted boats right up on the sand, gunning them full speed, scaring the sunbathers half to death. As the fishermen prepare to leave the boats on the beach, the sunbathers and street vendors gather around to check out the catch. The fishermen gather their fish, attach them to a pole, hoist the pole on their shoulders, and walk to the market.

If you're a potential customer, you have to decide what you want and how much you're willing to pay *before* they get to market, because in the twenty yards the fisherman has to walk, the price goes way up. If you don't beat the guy to the market, then suddenly the same fish is gonna have a whole different price tag attached to it. Hopefully, you'll get a good deal in the mad hustle.

The nice part about grilling this grouper is that the fish is not turned over. So the bottom of the grouper gets browned and the top gets beautifully steamed.

GROUPER Wrapped in BANANA LEAVES
WITH ROASTED PAPAYA SALSA

1 (4-pound) grouper, gutted and scaled

Salt and freshly ground black pepper

4 thin lime slices

4 small, thin onion slices

10 sprigs fresh cilantro, plus 3 tablespoons chopped

½ cup unsweetened coconut water

3 or 4 (20 by 14-inch) banana leaves, fresh or frozen (then thawed)

2 ripe papayas, halved lengthwise, seeded

1 large shallot, unpeeled

½ habanero chile, minced

3 tablespoons fresh lime juice

3 tablespoons olive oil

SERVES 4

A magnificent and not super-hard presentation: a large whole grouper wrapped in banana leaves and grilled with papaya halves. The leaves impart a smoky herbal flavor while protecting the fish. For those of you who have trouble finding a nice ripe papaya, my advice is to get a shack like I rent in Puerto Rico, then when the papaya is ripe it will fall off the tree and smash into the metal roof with a sound like a crashing meteorite. You will wake up thinking someone is shooting at the house. That would be a ripe papaya. If you don't have a corrugated roof or a Puerto Rican rental shack, feel the papaya. It should feel soft like your grandmother's arms. No, that might be too ripe, actually.

The nice part about grilling this grouper is that the fish is not turned over. So the bottom of the grouper gets browned and the top gets beautifully steamed.

(Put the grouper on a large rimmed baking sheet. Season inside and out with salt and pepper. Arrange the lime and onion slices in the cavity of the grouper along with the cilantro sprigs. Pour the coconut water inside the cavity and all over the grouper. Cover and refrigerate for at least 1 hour or up to 3 hours.

2 Light a hardwood charcoal fire. Working on the sheet pan, wrap the grouper in the banana leaves, starting at the tail end, keeping the cavity closed. Overlap the leaves so there are no bare spots and fold them around the grouper, keeping as much coconut water inside as possible. Fold all the leaves under the more thickly covered side of the grouper that will sit on the grill.

(recipe continues)

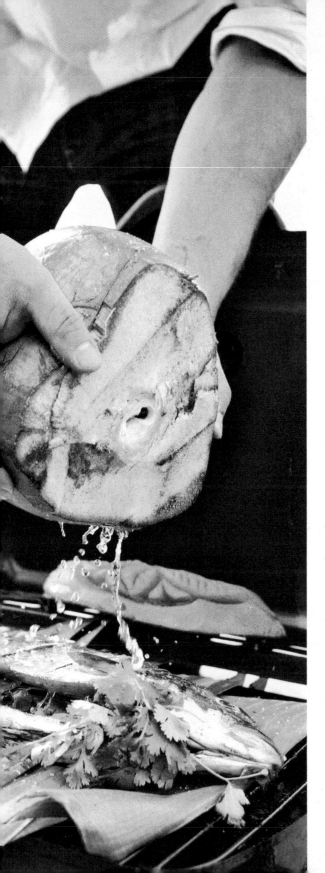

3   Make crosshatch cuts in the papayas. When the fire has burned down to a medium heat, carefully put the grouper on the grill, thick leafy side down. Put 2 of the papaya halves on top of the grouper and put the other 2 halves on the grill. Put the shallot on the grill and cover. Cook until the shallot is just tender, about 20 minutes. Cool, peel, and finely chop the shallot.

4   The grouper should be just cooked in 45 to 50 minutes. With 2 large spatulas, transfer the grouper to a clean large rimmed baking sheet and let rest for 10 to 15 minutes. Cut the flesh from the roasted papayas in chunks and place in a large bowl. Stir in the shallot, habanero, lime juice, olive oil, and chopped cilantro and season with salt and pepper.

5   Cut the banana leaves down the center of the grouper and open the leaves. With 2 forks, lift the meat from the grouper and place it on a large plate or platter. Lift the bones to get at the meat on the other side of the grouper and place that on the platter. Pour any juices over the grouper and serve with the salsa.

Bacon-Wrapped GROUPER FILLETS
WITH LEMON-GARLIC RELISH

This actually started out as a trout recipe, but I was in my shack in Puerto Rico with a plate full of grouper fillets one night as I was going over the recipes for this book and I thought, "What the heck, it's got bacon and garlic, it's got to be good with grouper." Guess what? It's good with almost every mild flaky fish and, dare I say, better with grouper!

1 tablespoon olive oil

2 large garlic cloves, thinly sliced

1 large lemon, peeled to the flesh, seeded, and finely chopped

Salt and freshly ground black pepper

12 strips bacon, not too thick

4 (6- to 8-ounce) grouper fillets, skinned

SERVES 4

1 In a medium skillet, heat the oil. Add the garlic and spread out. Cook over low heat until golden, about 1 minute. Add the chopped lemon and cook over medium heat until starting to soften, about 2 minutes. Let cool a bit and season with salt and pepper.

2 Wrap the bacon around the grouper neatly, in a slightly overlapping layer, and secure with toothpicks. Heat a large skillet and add the grouper. Cook over medium-high heat until the bacon is browned, about 4 minutes per side. Reduce the heat to medium if the bacon gets too dark before the fish is done. Put the grouper on plates, spoon the lemon relish over, and serve.

HALIBUT

Halibut are big. This makes them a good eating fish that produces a real meaty fillet; you can cut it two or three inches thick, like a steak. And—this is a big deal—when properly cooked, halibut has a moist flesh that flakes apart when you prod it with a fork. Nice!

I once fished for halibut with the Benkin family in Sitka, Alaska. We went about it the old-fashioned low-tech way. No big trawler for us, just a nice little Boston Whaler, riding through the gentle swells at sunset. We had set our long lines just as you would on a big commercial boat, the only difference being there were no mechanical winches to haul in our lines: It was all hand over hand. Tough work. I didn't see this getting any easier when I was introduced to my "helper."

"Wait a minute, how's this going to work?" I asked. "This little guy's going to do this?"

My "helper" was a five-year-old kid.

What I didn't understand was that this kid had been doing this his whole life. He could do everything that needed to be done on that boat. Kids in Alaska fly float planes and drive boats before they can drive a car. So yes, this kid was basically captain and fisherman all in one! This sounds ridiculous—but I pretty much learned everything I know about halibut fishing from a five-year-old kid. His only limitation was that he couldn't always get the fish *in* the boat because sometimes they were bigger than he was.

5247 C

38437

When I cook this on
the East Coast I do
it with fresh-picked
blueberries.

BLUEBERRY *Summer* HALIBUT
WITH HARISSA SAUCE & OYSTER MUSHROOMS

Colette Nelson, the chef at Ludvig's Bistro in Sitka, Alaska, made this for me, and it was, to use an overused but appropriate word, amazing! We picked our own huckleberries and caught our own fish. When I cook this on the East Coast I do it with fresh-picked blueberries. You can use a good white sturdy-fleshed fish like striped bass or even a big flounder if you are having a hard time finding sustainable halibut (by and large Alaskan is the most sustainable halibut, while East Coast stocks are definitely in danger). It's nice served over risotto.

2 cups fresh blueberries or huckleberries

¼ cup balsamic vinegar

¼ cup plus ⅓ cup Champagne or white wine

2½ tablespoons raw sugar

1 tablespoon or more harissa

1 large sprig fresh mint

Salt and freshly ground black pepper

2 tablespoons olive oil

1 pound oyster mushrooms, stems trimmed, caps halved

2 tablespoons vegetable oil

4 (6- to 8-ounce) halibut fillets, skinned

4 cups risotto, for serving

SERVES 4

In a large saucepan, combine the berries, vinegar, ¼ cup Champagne, the sugar, 1 tablespoon harissa, and mint sprig and bring to a simmer. Cook over medium-low heat, stirring often, until the berries break down, about 10 minutes. Set a coarse strainer over a bowl and strain the mixture, using a wooden spoon to push on the solids. Discard the solids and put the sauce back into the pan, adding a little more harissa if desired. Season with salt and pepper.

(recipe continues)

2 Preheat the oven to 400°F. In a large skillet, heat the olive oil. Add the mushrooms, stir well, and season with salt and pepper. Cover and cook over medium heat until the liquid from the mushrooms has evaporated and they brown, about 8 minutes.

3 In a large ovenproof skillet, heat the vegetable oil. Season the halibut with salt and pepper. Add the halibut to the skillet and cook over medium-high heat until browned, about 3 minutes. Turn the halibut and pour over the remaining ⅓ cup of Champagne. Put the skillet in the oven and bake until the halibut is just cooked, 3 to 4 minutes longer.

4 Reheat the sauce and mushrooms separately. Divide the risotto, if using, among 4 shallow bowls. Put the halibut on top along with the pan juices. Spoon the sauce and mushrooms over and serve.

HALIBUT CIOPPINO
WITH DUNGENESS CRAB

Cioppino is the catchall name for a tomato and wine-based fisherman's stew that originated with the Italian American fishing community in San Francisco Bay. It usually includes crab, which often makes for messy eating. I find that any time I eat crab if it's still in its shell, I end up with crab and sauce scattered all over my shirt. After all the mess, though, the Dungeness rewards you with large sweet claws and wide chambers of meat in the body, which are easy to get at. And your cioppino has to have halibut for its meatiness, which tends not to break up in the stew as more delicate fish might.

3 tablespoons olive oil

3 large garlic cloves, smashed and chopped

1 medium onion, diced

1 celery stalk, finely diced

⅛ teaspoon chile flakes

1 cup dry white wine

1 cup chopped canned tomatoes with juices

2 tablespoons Worcestershire sauce

1 bay leaf

1 cup Fish Stock (113) or clam juice

1 (2½-pound) Dungeness crab, quartered

1 pound skinned halibut fillet, cut into 2-inch chunks

Salt and freshly ground black pepper

¼ cup chopped fresh flat-leaf parsley

¼ cup chopped fresh basil

SERVES 4

1 In a large pot, warm the olive oil over medium heat. Add the garlic, onion, and celery, cover, and cook, stirring a few times, until golden, about 8 minutes. Add the chile flakes and cook for 1 minute. Add the wine and cook for 2 minutes. Add the tomatoes, Worcestershire, bay leaf, and stock and bring to a simmer. Add the quartered crab in an even layer, cover, and cook over low heat for 10 minutes. Turn over the crab quarters, cover, and cook until the crab is cooked through, 10 to 12 minutes longer. Discard the bay leaf.

2 Lift the crab quarters from the pot, place in a large bowl, and cover. Season the halibut chunks with salt and pepper and add to the pot. Simmer over low heat until the halibut is just cooked, about 4 minutes. Season with more salt and pepper. Put the crab back in the pot and cook 1 or 2 minutes, to heat through. Add the parsley and basil and serve in shallow bowls with nutcrackers to eat the crab.

One time I made a cioppino with a great chef in San Francisco. I was talking to him all about his "Italian" heritage and only at the end of cooking did he tell me he was actually Eastern European.

MACKEREL

Mackerel come in a number of shapes and sizes. Growing up, I would catch Boston mackerel in Menemsha, at the end of Martha's Vineyard. They were never very big: eight to ten inches. I would take home a bucket with four or five fish, and my proud mother would cook them up. Down South, Spanish mackerel fill the same niche and can be prepared just like Boston mackerel. Also in the South, you get king mackerel or kingfish, which is the super-size version of the Boston and Spanish species. It's a wonderful fish to fish for in the Florida Keys. It's as tasty as the little guys, just ten times bigger—maybe twenty times bigger. Think steak for the kings and a little veal cutlet for the smaller guys. To catch one is great fun because they come at you with such speed. Use any fresh bait if it's available; the kingfish is not a finicky eater.

I have always loved the taste of mackerel. Some people don't because it is an oily fish. Hey, fresh oil is good. It's only when it is exposed to the air for a long time and gets rancid that it's not good. Solution? Eat fresh fish that you catch yourself. It will taste super-good all the time.

I was eight years old the day I learned my biggest lesson about mackerel. I was sitting on the dock when a young girl with no shoes and crazy scraggly blonde hair sat down next to me. No doubt about it, she was my first crush. She started talking to me as she caught one mackerel after the next, and I felt like this was my opportunity to be a hero and teach her about preservation and not needing to take all these fish home.

Before I got the chance, she picked up her bucket of mackerel, and said, "Well, see you later." Why would one small girl need all those mackerel?, I wondered.

I thought she was going to take home all those fish to her parents and I guess eat 'em (like I always did). But I watched her as she went out to the end of the pier and pushed her way through four or five crusty old fishermen who were hogging the end. No doubt they were out for stripers and bluefish. She returned with the biggest friggin' striped bass I'd ever seen; it was as big as she was, and she could barely hold it, yet it took her all of fifteen minutes to land it. Pretty good! She dragged it back over the rocks, leaving me wide-eyed—and slightly in love for the first time.

Orange-Glazed KINGFISH STEAKS
WITH MANGO CHUTNEY

Finely grated zest of 1 orange

2 cups fresh pulpy orange juice, from 4 to 5 oranges

3 tablespoons honey

Salt and freshly ground black pepper

2 tablespoons olive oil

1 small red onion, finely diced

1 garlic clove, minced

1 red or orange bell pepper, cored, seeded, and cut into ½-inch dice

1 large ripe mango, peeled and cut into ½-inch dice

½ to 1 tablespoon habanero hot sauce

2 tablespoons vegetable oil

4 kingfish steaks, 1 to 1¼ inches thick

1 lime, cut into wedges

SERVES 4

Its full-flavored meat goes well with the zesty flavors of this recipe.

I love when the fishing boats come into Crash Boat Beach in Puerto Rico. Cool name. It's where the navy used to rescue downed airmen when they crashed on training flights. But I always like it because the fishermen drive their boats onto shore so fast they speed right up the sand. When these fishermen cut the massive kingfish into steaks, it's quite a scene, as their machetes flash in the sun and then whomp through the fish. Because the king mackerel is a narrow fish, it's not particularly suited to fillets. So steak it is! Its full-flavored meat goes well with the zesty flavors of this recipe.

1 In a small saucepan, combine all the orange zest, 1½ cups of the orange juice, and the honey and simmer over medium heat until reduced to ½ cup, about 10 minutes. Season with salt and pepper.

2 In a large skillet, heat the olive oil. Add the onion, garlic, and bell pepper, cover, and cook over medium heat until the vegetables start to soften, about 5 minutes. Add the mango and cook, stirring a few times, until the mango starts to soften, about 4 minutes. Add the remaining ½ cup of orange juice and cook for 1 minute. Add the hot sauce and remove from the heat. Season with salt and pepper.

3 In a very large nonstick skillet, heat the vegetable oil. Season the steaks with salt and pepper and add to the skillet. Cook over medium-high heat until browned, about 3 minutes per side. Reduce the heat to medium and cook the steaks 1 or 2 minutes longer until just cooked at the bone. Add the orange glaze and cook over medium-high heat, turning often, until the glaze reduces and the steaks are richly coated, about 1 minute.

4 Put the steaks on plates and spoon the mango chutney alongside. Drizzle with the remaining glaze and serve with lime wedges.

Tangy KINGFISH ESCABECHE

Escabeche is a fun word to say out loud. Before I knew what it meant I thought it would make a great nickname for a gangster, as in "Tony Escabeche, you don't mess with him." Actually it's a word that comes from Arabic via the Spanish, who loved to marinate fish in a sweet tangy brine known as escabeche. The large flake and rich taste of kingfish is perfect for the insanely spicy and nicely tangy marinade.

1 cup white vinegar, preferably cane vinegar

1 Scotch bonnet chile, thinly sliced

Salt and freshly ground black pepper

20 pimento or allspice berries

10 black peppercorns

Pinch of sugar

1 medium onion, sliced ¼ inch thick

1 medium carrot, sliced almost paper thin

Vegetable oil, for frying

4 kingfish steaks, about 1½ inches thick, 10 to 12 ounces each

SERVES 4

1   In a medium saucepan, combine the vinegar, Scotch bonnet chile, ¼ cup of water, 1 teaspoon salt, the pimento berries, peppercorns, sugar, onion, and carrot and bring to a boil. Simmer for 5 minutes.

2   In a large skillet, heat ¼ inch of oil. Season the steaks with salt and pepper and add to the pan. Cook over medium-high heat until a very brown crust forms, about 3 minutes per side. The fish should barely be cooked at the bone. Transfer the steaks to a shallow dish large enough for them to fit in one layer. Pour the hot marinade over and let cool to room temperature. The fish can marinate for up to 2 hours at room temperature or you can refrigerate it overnight. Serve at room temperature or lightly chilled.

The marinade can be refrigerated for up to 1 week.

Lupe's SPANISH MACKEREL
WITH SAUTÉED MUSHROOMS & PROVOLONE

At the Williamsburg Diner, now long gone, my friend the Italian chef Massimo would pretend he didn't hear you if you asked for grated cheese on one of his seafood pastas! I don't understand where this whole no-cheese-with-seafood thing came from. As far as I am concerned it's one more lame old rule made to be broken, or at least questioned. Though not to him . . . I was way too terrified of him. For sure, this recipe proves, at least in the case of provolone and mackerel, that good things happen when you combine the two. Spanish mackerel is actually quite mild and tender for a mackerel. The skin is so thin, there's no point in trying to cut it away. It fries up very nice and crisp, too. You may substitute Boston mackerel.

3 tablespoons olive oil

1 pound white mushrooms, sliced ¼ inch thick

Salt and freshly ground black pepper

2 tablespoons unsalted butter

2 large shallots, thinly sliced

¼ cup plus 2 tablespoons white wine

2 tablespoons fresh lime juice

4 (6-ounce) Spanish mackerel fillets, or Boston mackerel

Mayonnaise, for spreading

1 cup Italian bread crumbs

Vegetable oil, for shallow frying

4 thin slices provolone cheese

SERVES 4

1   In a large skillet, heat the olive oil. Add the mushrooms, season with salt and pepper, and stir well. Cover and cook over medium heat, stirring a few times, until the mushroom liquid has evaporated and they are browned, about 8 minutes. Add 1 tablespoon of the butter and stir in the shallots. Cover and cook until the shallots are soft and start to brown, about 5 minutes. Add the wine and simmer for 1 minute. Add the lime juice, cover, and remove from the heat.

2   Season the mackerel with salt and pepper and coat with a thin layer of mayonnaise. Pat the bread crumbs onto the mackerel to coat completely. In a large cast-iron skillet, heat ⅛ inch of vegetable oil until very hot. Add the mackerel and cook over medium-high heat until browned and crisp, about 3 minutes. Reduce the heat to medium if it browns too quickly. Turn and cook until the fish is just done and browned on the other side, about 3 minutes longer.

3   Meanwhile, preheat the broiler. Reheat the mushrooms, season with salt and pepper, and stir in the remaining 1 tablespoon of butter to blend. Spoon the mushroom topping over the fried mackerel. Top each portion with a slice of provolone and broil until melted. Serve right away.

MAHIMAHI!

Not too many years ago, this fish was known as dolphin, but when people began to think that they were being served the intelligent mammals they saw on nature documentaries, they were justifiably very upset. So to get rid of this unfortunate confusion, it became common practice to refer to dolphin fish as mahi, short for mahimahi, the Hawaiian word for "very strong." They're such a beautiful, brilliantly colored tropical fish, that sometimes I can't believe I'm allowed to catch these things. They are that beautiful. They're also aggressive, fast swimmers, and have a lot of muscle on them, so they are super-fun to catch.

One of the fun things about mahi is the way they will congregate under patches of sea grass, floating in open water. Once you hook a mahi, bring it almost to the surface but don't take it from the water. Other mahi will be attracted by the commotion and you can catch one after another as long as you keep that first guy busy. When you do land a mahi, watch how it changes color in front of you: beautiful yellows and aqua and deep blue. Kind of a final light show before the kill.

Mahimahi is a good starter fish for perfecting fillet technique. The skin itself is easy to pierce, and because the bones are solid, you never have to stop and ask yourself, "What is that? Am I into bone? Am I not into bone?" The mahimahi has a really nice, prominent backbone, and it's easy to glide your knife up the vertebrae and come down on the other side of the backbone at an angle to get at the meat.

Beautiful, fun to catch, easy to fillet—what more could you want? And oh yeah, one more thing: it's super-delicious.

PLANTAIN-CRUSTED MAHIMAHI WITH PINEAPPLE SALSA

This is such a fun dish that I was asked to make it for Kathie Lee and Hoda on the *Today* show. The only trick to this is making sure you get the temp just right on your pan so that the crust is golden brown and flavorful while the fish is cooked through but moist. You know how when you make pancakes, you start out by testing one to make sure the pan is at the right heat? That's what I do with the mahi here. If I have enough fish I set one fillet aside as a test fillet so I can work on achieving that golden-brown crisp shell with the plantain chips. A slightly thinner fillet is good for this recipe.

1 small garlic clove, minced

Salt

3 tablespoons olive oil

½ medium red onion, finely diced and rinsed with cold water, drained

Finely grated zest of 1 lime

¼ cup fresh lime juice

2 cups ½-inch diced pineapple

2 tomatillos, husked, washed and dried, and cut into eighths

1 large plum tomato, cut into ½-inch dice

1 small red bell pepper, cored, seeded, and cut into ¼-inch dice

1 small green bell pepper, cored, seeded, and cut into ¼-inch dice

1 serrano or jalapeño, minced

6 (6-ounce) mahimahi fillets, skinned

2 eggs, beaten

1 cup plantain chips, finely crushed with a rolling pin

Vegetable oil, for frying

SERVES 4 TO 6

In a large bowl, combine the garlic with a pinch of salt and 1 tablespoon of the olive oil and let stand for 5 minutes. Add the onion, lime zest, and the remaining 2 tablespoons of olive oil. Let stand for 5 minutes. Add the lime juice, pineapple, tomatillos, tomato, red and green bell peppers, and the serrano and mix well. Season with salt.

(recipe continues)

2 Season the mahimahi with salt. Put the eggs and plantain chips in separate shallow bowls. Dip the fish in the egg, letting excess drip off. Then dredge the fish in the chips to coat well.

3 In 2 large skillets, heat ¼ inch of vegetable oil until shimmering. Cook the fish in the skillets, leaving some room between each piece for even cooking. Cook over medium-high heat for 1 minute. Reduce the heat to medium and cook until browned and crisp, about 3 minutes. Turn the fish and cook about 4 minutes or longer, until the fish flakes and the other side is crisp. Adjust the heat as needed if the crust starts to brown too quickly.

4 Place the fish on plates and pass the pineapple salsa at the table.

MAHI CEVICHE
WITH GRAPEFRUIT, TOASTED COCONUT & ROASTED PEANUTS

Ceviche is a form of "cooking" fish in the acid of citrus fruits that is popular all through Central America and reaches its pinnacle in Ecuador and Peru. Actually the proper term for the process is *acidulation*, but it has the same effect on fish flesh as cooking. Mahi is ideal for ceviche. It has a firm texture that doesn't fall apart when the grapefruit juice tenderizes it. It is easy to cut into a neat dice, and it has a mild, appealing flavor. Mahi is great with this combination of fruity and fiery tastes and the crunchy texture of peanut and coconut. It's positively, deliciously killer.

2 teaspoons finely grated grapefruit zest

½ teaspoon finely grated lime zest

¼ cup fresh grapefruit juice

2 tablespoons fresh lime juice

1 scallion, finely chopped

1 Thai chile, finely chopped

2 teaspoons sugar

½ teaspoon salt

½ teaspoon freshly ground black pepper

¾ pound mahimahi fillet, cut into ½-inch pieces

1 sweet star fruit, half cut into ½-inch pieces, half sliced for garnish (optional)

Toasted coconut, for garnish

Roasted peanuts, chopped, for garnish

SERVES 4
as an appetizer

1 In a large bowl, combine the grapefruit and lime zests and juices. Stir in the scallion, chile, sugar, salt, and pepper. Stir in the mahimahi and coat thoroughly with the citrus marinade. Cover and refrigerate, stirring a few times, for at least 1 hour and up to 4 hours.

2 Just before serving, stir in the star fruit pieces and divide among 4 bowls. Garnish with star fruit slices, if using. Top with toasted coconut and peanuts and serve.

AN All American FISH FRY

This is a catchall recipe that folks who fish the ponds in the South and Midwest often make with the mixed bag they usually collect from a day's fishing. I have had it from Iowa to Georgia to Tennessee. In the same way that Frenchmen make bouillabaisse and Italians make brodetto with whatever fish is on hand, all those little guys like bluegills, crappie, and perch form the basis of many wonderful fish frys. Not only do these panfish make good eating, but they remove some of the competition in a lake or pond where they compete with the more glamorous and fun bass. Not to take anything away from the little fellows, though. It really is fun to catch them, especially with kids. Then you clean 'em, bread 'em, and fry 'em up. With some Hush Puppies (page 243) and Kale & Cabbage Slaw (page 237) on the side, you have yourself a bona fide party.

¾ cup all-purpose flour

¾ cup fine cornmeal

1 tablespoon fine salt

1 tablespoon garlic powder

2 teaspoons cayenne pepper

2 teaspoons freshly ground black pepper

2 teaspoons chili powder

2½ quarts vegetable oil

12 assorted whole small freshwater fish, 4 to 8 ounces each, such as crappie, bluegill, sunnies, and perch, gutted and scaled

Lemon wedges, for serving

SERVES 6

1 In a large heavy brown paper bag, combine the flour, cornmeal, salt, garlic powder, cayenne pepper, black pepper, and chili powder. Shake the bag to thoroughly blend the seasonings.

2 Preferably over an outdoor gas burner, pour the oil into a 4- to 6-quart heavy-duty Dutch oven or enameled cast-iron pot and heat to 375°F. Have a large rack set over a large, rimmed baking sheet near the oil. Put 3 fish in the bag and make sure to completely coat the cavities of the fish with the seasonings to help add more flavor and prevent splatters from the moisture in the cavities. Now shake the bag and coat the fish all over.

3 Add the 3 seasoned fish to the hot oil and fry, turning a few times, about 4 minutes for the smaller fish and 6 minutes for the larger fish. With a large slotted spoon or spatula, drain the fish on the rack and repeat with the remaining fish and seasonings. Serve right away with lemon wedges.

PORGY

In Massachusetts, the fish that my Brooklyn fishing buddies call porgy is what we call scup. No local fish is more delicately flaky or sweet-fleshed. I fished for them my whole life, but I always thought of them as bycatch, something I'd run into when looking for bigger fish. I don't have any special bait I use for porgy; they'll eat just about anything offered to them. I've caught them on squid and bits of mackerel or shrimp and even on bits of porgy. They are white-fleshed little guys that are great bait when you're after bigger fish, and when the bigger game don't bite, the porgy make a fine meal instead. In fancy restaurants these days they call them sea bream or dourade and charge up to thirty dollars an order. The markup is insanely good.

Although porgy can grow to five pounds, I usually catch one-pounders, perfect to fry or roast whole. Because they are smaller and you can catch a lot of them at one time (they tend to school in groups), they have a reputation for being easy. As with many things in life, they are easy if you know how. They also make a fine fisherman's meal when you are spending a day on the water sailing or pleasure-boating and you just want to throw a line over and catch dinner. Porgies caught this way have been my après-sailing supper many times over the years.

I've prepared porgy as sashimi on crackers or with just a little bit of lime and beer. Sometimes I'll use a serrano pepper or a jalapeño if it's around. What I'm saying is that they are a good all-around eating fish.

Grilled WHOLE PORGIES
WITH SMOKY TOMATO CHUTNEY

This is a great way to cook the not very large, and therefore not always worth filleting, porgy. The skin gets super-crisp and the flesh is easy to eat because it flakes off the bone—then you just lift up the backbone and presto! You have another whole boneless fillet to eat. Porgies are also great to grill because they cook up quickly. I have cooked fresh-caught porgies on the little grill I keep on my boat. This is an amazing dish to make right there with very few ingredients, especially when washed down with a mucho cold cerveza or your favorite warm-weather cocktail.

2 large jalapeños

2 tablespoons olive oil, plus more for coating

1 large shallot, thinly sliced

1 garlic clove, thinly sliced

½ teaspoon smoked sweet paprika

½ teaspoon ground cumin

5 plum tomatoes (1¼ pounds), chopped

¼ cup clam juice

¼ cup fresh orange juice

1 tablespoon fresh lime juice

Salt and freshly ground black pepper

4 (1-pound) porgies, gutted and scaled

SERVES 4

1. Over a gas flame or under a broiler, lightly char the jalapeños all over, turning, until the skin can be pulled off. Let cool, then peel off the charred skin. Halve and seed the jalapeños.

2. In a medium skillet, heat 2 tablespoons of olive oil. Add the shallot and cook over medium heat until caramelized, about 5 minutes. Add the garlic, paprika, and cumin, and cook until fragrant, about 1 minute. Add the tomatoes, clam juice, orange juice, lime juice, and jalapeños, and cook over medium heat, stirring a few times, until chunky, 6 to 8 minutes. Season with salt and pepper.

3. Clean and oil a grill well, then light. Coat the porgies generously with olive oil and season with salt and pepper. Put the porgies on the grill, cover, and grill over medium-high heat until the skin is nicely charred. Don't move the porgies too soon; let a crisp, lightly charred crust develop before trying to lift from the grill with a spatula. The porgies should come off the grate easily when the spatula is gently pushed under the skin and then lifted up. Use your hand to hold the uncooked top of each porgy as you flip it over. The first side should take about 8 minutes, the second side about 5 minutes longer. Serve right away with the chutney.

The chutney can be refrigerated overnight. Serve at cool room temperature.

Salt-Baked WHOLE PORGY
WITH COCKTAIL ONION SAUCE

Salt crusting is one of the most foolproof ways to make juicy fish with a beautiful flake. Because the salt casing completely seals in the fish, no moisture can escape. You have to try really hard to overcook a fish with this very forgiving method. I find that the way to achieve perfection is to insert a thermometer into the thickest part of the fish before putting it in the oven. Cook to an internal temperature of 125°F to 130°F. The cocktail onions perk up each mouthful with just the right amount of tangy crunch.

8 bay leaves

8 fresh thyme sprigs

4 whole porgies, gutted and scaled, fins and tails trimmed, about ½ pound each

6 cups (3 pounds) kosher or other good-quality, slightly coarse salt

1 small jar cocktail onions, drained and sliced in half

3 tablespoons white wine vinegar

¼ cup olive oil or melted, unsalted butter

Salt and freshly ground black pepper

SERVES 4

1 Preheat the oven to 500°F or light a very hot fire in a grill, set up for indirect cooking. Put the bay leaves and thyme in the porgy cavities and secure with toothpicks.

2 In separate baking dishes or 1 large, wide one that holds all the porgies with space in between, put 3 cups of the kosher salt. Spread it out in a thick layer roughly the size of each porgy, and sprinkle with water until damp. Put a porgy in the center of the salt layer, or evenly space them in the large dish, and press lightly to fit. Add the remaining 3 cups salt on top and pack it in to cover the fish. Sprinkle more water and pat well to form a mummy-like case for the porgy, making sure to cover all parts of the fish.

3 Bake in the oven or opposite the coals in the covered grill, turning the pans once or twice, for about 12 minutes. Stick a meat thermometer through the salt and into the fish. If the fish is not done, pat the salt back over and continue to cook for 3 to 4 minutes longer.

4 In a bowl, stir the onions and vinegar with the olive oil to make a glossy sauce. If using butter, add just before serving. Season with salt and pepper.

5 Have the plates ready. Crack the crust, lifting off large pieces of crust, and brush off as much salt as possible from the fish. With two forks, lift the porgies from the crust and put them on plates. Using a paper towel, wipe all the salt off the porgies and with a fork, start at the tail and roll the skin up on the fork as you go. Pass the cocktail onion sauce to spoon over.

SALMON

Salmon is probably the most popular fish on restaurant menus, and on banquet tables, where too often, however, it can be cooked to the consistency of a dry dish towel. But a fresh-caught salmon is one of nature's treasures. I have fished for salmon a number of ways: on flies, with spinning equipment, and even with my bare hands. I am a little conflicted, though, about salmon. They are often overfished and farming practices aren't always the most sustainable or environmentally sound. However, in Alaska they are well managed for both anglers and commercial fishers.

One day I went fishing for salmon on the Kenai, one of Alaska's best and most productive salmon fisheries. It was on a part of the river accessible only by float plane. Once I jumped off the plane, I hoped my guide would be there, waiting in a little flat-bottomed boat, because if he wasn't, I'd be a prime target for the area's bears, which are everywhere. But thankfully, my guy, armed with a shotgun and a revolver, picked me up on time.

My plan was to fly-fish, but these particular salmon at this time of year were not taking flies. I could tell I wasn't pissing off the salmon enough to get them to take but I was pissing myself off plenty by being stubborn. My guide wanted me to switch to lures but I kept saying, "Dude, I came here to fly-fish, I came here to fly-fish!" Finally, I bowed to the inevitable. The only things the salmon were going for were shiny spinners, and very reluctantly, I switched over. Sure enough, once I switched to the spinning equipment, the bite was on! My mood went from stubborn and unfulfilled to successful and happy. I forgot all about fly-fishing for the moment.

We caught our personal limit (the law allowed more, but I saw no need to fill my cooler with fish that I was never going to eat just because I could). We filleted them right there on the side of the river, tossing the carcasses to feed the bears. As an extra treat, I fixed up some fresh roe with sea salt and ate it on saltine crackers. My guide took the fish, slathered it in honey, wrapped it in aluminum foil, and threw it on the grill. It was simple and beyond delicious! At around this time a young moose came by for a visit. And by visit I mean head-down, running straight at me.

IS A SALMON A SALMON?

There is much to be said about salmon, so let me try to simplify. Wild Atlantic salmon, the only true salmon, is borderline endangered and is rarely if ever available in markets. Too bad, because it's great.

That leaves the Pacific salmon, which are really not true salmon; but unless you are another salmon, you would be hard-pressed to tell the difference between these fish and their distant cousins in the Atlantic.

The chinook or king salmon have ruby-red flesh and high fat content (good fat, omega 3's). Many people think they are rightly called king because they are so delicious.

Coho salmon or silver salmon, so called because of the color of their skin, have bright red flesh and a delicate texture but are just about as full-flavored as kings.

Sockeye (aka red salmon) have deep dark color and flavor. They are not as highly prized by some gourmets, but I hope I am never accused of being a gourmet.

Smoky SALMON CHOWDER
WITH PUMPKIN

1 (2-pound) acorn squash, halved horizontally, seeds scooped out

¼ cup olive oil

Salt and freshly ground black pepper

4 tablespoons (½ stick) unsalted butter

2 medium leeks, white and pale green parts, sliced crosswise ½ inch wide

1 large red or yellow bell pepper, cored, seeded, and cut into ½-inch-thick strips

1 tablespoon finely grated peeled fresh ginger

¼ to ½ teaspoon chile flakes

2 tablespoons all-purpose flour

3 cups clam juice

3 cups vegetable stock (homemade or store-bought)

1 teaspoon chopped fresh thyme

1 teaspoon chopped fresh marjoram

6 saffron threads, crumbled

1 cup heavy cream

1 (15-ounce) can pure pumpkin puree

1½ pounds salmon fillet with skin

2 tablespoons fresh lemon juice

2 tablespoons chopped fresh dill

¾ cup shredded high-quality smoked gouda, such as Taylor Farms

Lemon wedges, for serving

SERVES 6 TO 8

Pumpkin, salmon, and smoked cheese: This is a dish made to simmer in a cauldron over a wood fire in a pine grove on the shore. Even if you can't go for the whole outdoorsy nine yards, it still has an aura of deep forest when you make it in the kitchen. And even though you roast the squash in the oven, they are especially great when finished on a hot grill. I make this chowder often in Vermont, where I can get a beautiful smoked gouda from a local farm. This gives a wonderful smoky flavor to the chowder, and if you can find maple-smoked gouda, you are in the sweet spot!

Preheat the oven to 350°F. Rub the cut sides of the squash with 2 tablespoons of olive oil, and season with salt and pepper. Place them cut side down on a large rimmed baking sheet. Bake for about 50 minutes, or until they are just tender but still hold their shape. Turn the squash cut side up and let it cool. Carefully scoop out the flesh in large pieces. Cut the squash into 1-inch chunks. Reserve the acorn squash shells, if desired, for serving.

(recipe continues)

2 In a large pot, melt the butter. Add the leeks, bell pepper, and ginger and cook over medium-low heat, covered, stirring a few times, until softened, about 8 minutes. Stir in the chile flakes and cook for 1 minute. Stir in the flour. Slowly whisk in the clam juice until smooth, then stir in the stock. Bring to a boil over medium-high heat, whisking, until the soup simmers and thickens. Reduce the heat to low, add the thyme, marjoram, and saffron, and simmer, stirring occasionally, for 30 minutes. Stir in the cream and pumpkin puree and simmer, stirring often, for about 5 minutes to heat through.

3 Meanwhile, rub the salmon with the remaining 2 tablespoons of olive oil and season with salt and pepper. Sprinkle with the lemon juice and dill, and let stand for at least 10 minutes or up to 20 minutes.

4 Light a charcoal grill. Grill the salmon, skin side down, over a hot fire, covered, until medium rare, 8 to 10 minutes. With 2 long spatulas lift the salmon from the grill, sliding the spatulas under the skin and placing the fish on a platter. Let the salmon rest for 5 to 10 minutes.

5 Reheat the soup to a simmer and whisk in the cheese. Cook over low heat, whisking, until the cheese melts, 2 to 3 minutes. Do not let the soup boil. Remove from the heat, stir in the squash cubes, and season with salt and pepper.

6 Ladle the soup into bowls or the acorn squash shells. Lift the salmon from the skin, discarding the skin, and flake the salmon into each soup. Serve with lemon wedges.

GRILLED GRAVLAX

This is a brining technique well known to all Nordic peoples. Gravlax is produced by a quick cure in salt, sugar, and dill. I prefer the fattier sockeye here over other wild salmon such as coho, because a very lean salmon does not work well for this dish. Plus, the color is enough to knock your socks off. I put this gravlax on my bagel and I'm a happy man! This is totally fun to do at home and kinda impressive and cool, if you ask me.

¼ cup kosher salt

5 tablespoons, packed, light brown sugar

1 cup chopped fresh dill

4 (8-ounce) center-cut salmon fillets with skin

1 cup dry white wine

Vegetable oil

Lemon wedges, for serving

Horseradish Cream Sauce (recipe follows)

SERVES 4

1 In a small bowl, blend together the salt and brown sugar, rubbing the sugar into the salt to get rid of lumps. Add the dill. Put the salmon fillets in a large shallow dish that fits them evenly in one layer. Rub some of the salt-sugar mixture into the skin and flesh sides and set the fillets skin side down. Sprinkle the rest of the mixture over the tops of the fillets. Cover and refrigerate for 1½ hours.

2 Rinse the fillets under cold water, rinse out the dish, and put the fillets back in the dish. Add the wine and turn the fillets in the wine, setting them skin side up. Cover and refrigerate for 1 hour.

3 Light a grill. Pat the fillets dry with paper towels and drizzle with oil to coat the skin and flesh. Oil the grill and set the fillets skin side down on the grill so the fillets run at a 90-degree angle to the grates on the grill. Grill the fillets until the skin is nicely charred and crisp, about 3 minutes. When the skin is properly crisp, the spatula can then be run under the fillets, going with the direction of the grates to remove the fish without tearing. Turn the fillets and grill 2 to 3 minutes longer, until the salmon is medium to medium-rare.

4 Serve the fillets, crisp skin side up, with lemon wedges and the horseradish cream sauce.

HORSERADISH CREAM SAUCE

¼ cup mayonnaise

½ cup sour cream

2 to 3 tablespoons jarred
horseradish, drained

2 tablespoons chopped
fresh flat-leaf parsley or dill

Salt and freshly ground
black pepper

**MAKES ABOUT
1 CUP**

Horseradish, with its combination of sweetness
and sharpness, wakes up the taste buds big-time.
Look for jarred horseradish in fish markets
or at the fish counter of your market, as that
will usually be fresher and stronger than shelf
brands. But in a pinch, the store-bought stuff
will do fine.

In a small bowl, blend the mayonnaise, sour cream,
horseradish, and parsley and season with salt and pepper.

*The sauce can be refrigerated for up to 5 days.
Stir well before serving.*

PAN-ROASTED SALMON
DUSTED WITH SPICES & HERBS

This is the very first recipe in *The Elements of Taste*, a classic cookbook that Peter Kaminsky wrote with the legendary chef Gray Kunz. The idea was simple, the execution easy. Rather than making a complex sauce or going through complicated cooking steps, they decided to cook the salmon as simply as possible and then make it special by dusting it with a custom spice mix and a salad of finely chopped fresh herbs. It was one of the greatest hits in that book and it's now in my basic repertoire. I've tried it with striper and weakfish, too. Equally good.

Spices and herbs

1½ tablespoons kosher salt

⅛ teaspoon cayenne pepper

¼ teaspoon ground cardamom

½ teaspoon ground nutmeg

½ teaspoon coarsely ground white pepper

2 tablespoons minced fresh chives

½ cup finely chopped fresh flat-leaf parsley

½ cup finely chopped fresh mint

½ cup finely chopped fresh dill

Salmon

1 tablespoon vegetable oil

4 (6-ounce) salmon fillets, about 1 to 1½ inches thick, with skin

Salt and coarsely ground white pepper

Cayenne pepper

1 tablespoon unsalted butter, cut into small pieces

SERVES 4

1 To prepare the spices and herbs: In a small bowl, combine the salt, cayenne pepper, cardamom, nutmeg, and white pepper. In another small bowl, combine the chives, parsley, mint, and dill.

2 To make the salmon: Preheat the oven to 325°F. In a large ovenproof skillet, heat the oil until shimmering. Add the salmon, skin side down, and cook over medium heat until the skin is crisp, about 2 minutes. Season the salmon with salt, white pepper, and cayenne pepper and dot all over with the butter pieces.

3 Transfer the skillet to the oven and bake for about 4 minutes. The salmon should be rare on the inside and medium-well around the edges. Remove the skillet from the oven.

4 Place the salmon fillets on a platter and sprinkle with the herb mixture. Lightly dust the salmon with some spice mixture and serve.

I've tried it with striper and weakfish, too. Equally good.

I've caught sardines commercially in the cold Pacific waters of northern California. It's one of the biggest fisheries in the United States, which is ironic considering they're one of the smallest fish around. I once went out on a gigantic hundred-foot converted military vessel, with four or five wells. These boats are equipped to go out for days at a time to pack the wells until they're brimming with sardines. The equipment is pretty pricey and high-tech: a 200- or 400-horsepower engine inside the boat, with 200-yard-long nets called purse seines and electronic fish finders. All of this is wielded by a wonderfully efficient crew who intricately sets the nets. Once the fish finder picks up on a promising upcoming patch of fish—and I'm talking thousands of fish—a signal blares on deck, and it becomes a race in which every crew member runs on deck, jumping over rope, hurrying to set the net and cast it wide enough to enclose the entire school of sardines. They know that if they mess up or if something goes wrong, the whole school will escape.

There is one guy who is the key player. The crew drops this guy in a boat twelve feet into the water; he free-falls for a second before hitting the water and racing off in the skiff to set the net in a big circle around the fish. Then of course there's the tricky business of lifting the fish from the net into the boat, which is not easy because the net has to be closed up tight enough to fit through a funnel on the side of the boat. It's a challenging, dirty, and race-to-beat-the-clock experience. To add to the complication, you're dealing with sea lions, seals, and all those other non-fishy creatures that get caught in your net that you do not want to eat or harm. Meanwhile, the sea lions and seals are just delighted that you've corralled all the fish for them; they're what I like to call "uninvited dinner guests."

SARDINE SKEWERS
WITH THAI DIPPING SAUCE

I wasn't always the biggest fan of sardines. I grew up hating the kinds of sardines that came in a tin or were pickled. Once I ate fresh sardines at restaurants, though, I was hooked. At a tiny restaurant in San Diego, I learned how to best prepare them. First we cleaned them, just as you would a big fish. Then we gutted and scaled them. They have these teeny tiny little scales that you can pull off with your fingers, and then you stick 'em on a skewer—adding a little bit of oil, salt, and pepper—and put them on the grill. I've added a few different ingredients of my own, but it all started in San Diego. I love to do these little guys on the beach over an open fire. You can make the dipping sauce ahead of time and pack it up to take to the beach.

12 large fresh sardines, gutted and scaled

Vegetable oil

Salt

4 garlic cloves, minced

2 tablespoons minced peeled fresh ginger

Juice of 2 limes

¼ cup fish sauce

1 tablespoon sugar

1 Thai chile, minced

2 tablespoons chopped fresh cilantro

2 tablespoons chopped fresh mint

SERVES 4

1 Soak 12 bamboo skewers in water for 20 minutes. Thread each sardine on a skewer lengthwise, along the stomach, to keep the fish intact. Rub with oil and season lightly with salt.

2 In a small bowl, combine the garlic, ginger, lime juice, fish sauce, sugar, chile, cilantro, and mint.

3 Light a grill. Grill the sardines over a hot fire for about 2 minutes per side, until nicely charred and just cooked, turning very carefully, as they have a tendency to fall apart easily. Put the sardines on plates, and pass the dipping sauce at the table.

Go-To SARDINE SANDWICH
WITH FRIED EGGPLANT & CHERRY TOMATOES

4 large sardines, about 3 ounces each

2½ tablespoons olive oil

1 medium onion, sliced ¼ inch thick

Salt and freshly ground black pepper

½ pound narrow eggplant, cut into 8 (¼-inch-thick) slices

1 tablespoon Dijon mustard

½ tablespoon mayonnaise, plus more for spreading

½ cup panko bread crumbs

Vegetable oil, for frying

10 cherry tomatoes, halved

4 (⅓-inch-thick) slices Tuscan bread, about 9 inches wide, halved crosswise

4 (⅛-inch-thick) slices Manchego or aged gouda cheese, about 2 inches wide

SERVES 4

I love fish sandwiches. Some small fish are perfectly suited to be sandwiched and the sardine is definitely in that club. I love the way they look when I fry them up and stick 'em in a sandwich and their little tails stick out. This sandwich was a happy accident. I had some great fried sardines kicking around from the night before and come lunchtime I was hungry for them again. Hey, did I say I *love* fish sandwiches?

Cut the heads off of the sardines. Take a thin, sharp knife and cut down either side of the sardine ribs, cutting them from the spines without digging too deep into the flesh. Cut down either side of the remaining spines all the way to the tail. Tap the knife on the spine just before the tail and snap off the spine, leaving the tail intact. Run your fingers down the spine from the tail to the head end to loosen the meat from the bone. Starting at the tail, pull out the spine from the sardines while pressing the meat to keep it intact, then discard the spines. Hold the knife at the top of one of the side rib cages and glide the knife just under the rib bones, cutting them down and off, while leaving as much meat as possible on the sardines. Refrigerate the sardines.

2   In a large cast-iron skillet, heat 1 tablespoon of the olive oil. Add the onion, season with salt and pepper, cover, and cook over medium heat, stirring a few times, until browned and soft, about 7 minutes. Transfer the onion to a medium bowl. Add the remaining 1½ tablespoons of olive oil to the skillet and when hot, add the eggplant slices and turn them to coat both sides with the oil. Season with salt and pepper and cook over medium-low heat until browned and soft, about 3 minutes per side. Transfer the eggplant to the bowl of onion. Reserve the skillet.

3   In a small bowl, mix together the mustard and mayonnaise. Season the sardines with salt and pepper, then spread the mustard mixture on both sides. Put the panko crumbs in a shallow bowl and while holding the sardines by the tail, pat the crumbs onto the sardines. Heat ⅛ inch of vegetable oil in the reserved skillet and when shimmering, add the sardines, boned side down. Cook over medium-high heat until golden brown and crisp, about 2 minutes. Turn the sardines and cook over medium heat until browned and crisp, about 1 minute longer. Drain on paper towels.

4   Pour off most of the oil, leaving just a shiny coating. Add the tomatoes and cook, stirring a few times, until the tomatoes give off some juices. Put 4 of the bread halves in the skillet on medium heat and place a piece of cheese on each. Put the onion over the cheese and then place a fried sardine over, with the tail sticking out the rounded end of the bread. Next, place 2 eggplant slices. Close the sandwiches and cook over medium heat until toasted, about 2 minutes per side. Lift 1 of the slices of bread, spread a little mayonnaise, close the sandwiches, and serve with the sautéed tomatoes.

SARDINES Wrapped in FIG LEAVES
WITH TOMATOES & CAPERS

If you live in a region where fig leaves are readily available, use them, because they are wonderful for cooking fish. They have a slightly lemony taste and make a sturdy wrap. They also crisp up nicely on the grill. If you pick the leaves yourself, keep in mind that fig leaves are easy to find and identify, but look out for poison ivy that may be growing nearby! On Martha's Vineyard the two plants often grow near one another and, speaking from experience, if you don't watch out when picking fig leaves, I can pretty much guarantee you a dose of poison ivy. But enough about that. Here we have a superb grilling fish with the flavor power to stand up to charring, the tang of capers, and the smoky sweetness of ripe tomatoes. You can substitute large tomatillos for the tomatoes for an even tangier filling.

4 plum tomatoes

1 large garlic clove, minced

1 tablespoon capers, drained and chopped

2 tablespoons olive oil, plus more for coating and drizzling

Pinch of chile flakes

Salt and freshly ground black pepper

12 sardines, about 3 ounces each, boned (see Go-To Sardine Sandwich with Fried Eggplant & Cherry Tomatoes, page 190)

36 medium-size fresh fig or grape leaves, stemmed

SERVES 4

1 Light a grill. Put the tomatoes over a hot fire and grill until charred all over. Let cool, then discard the skins. Finely chop the tomatoes and place in a medium bowl. Stir in the garlic, capers, 2 tablespoons of olive oil, and the chile flakes, and season with salt and pepper.

2 Open up the sardines, skin side down, and season with salt and pepper. Divide the tomato mixture among the sardines, spreading it over one side of the fillet. Close the sardines and drizzle with olive oil. Rub the fig leaves on both sides with olive oil. Lay out a fig leaf and place a sardine, tail end on the wide side of the leaf. Wrap the leaf around the sardine and interlock another fig leaf while wrapping around the sardine, using one more leaf if needed to enclose the fish. Drizzle with more olive oil and smooth the leaves over the sardines. Repeat with the remaining sardines, filling, and fig leaves.

3 Grill the sardines over a hot fire until the fig leaves are nicely charred and crisp, about 2 minutes per side. Serve right away.

SNAKE-HEAD

I once worked for the New York State Department of Environmental Conservation on a survey of fish populations in New York City water. We had heard that snakeheads, which are not native to America, had entered a shallow body of water near Flushing Meadow, Queens (that's as far as I am going to go in revealing a fishing hole). We were electro-fishing, a standard procedure whereby a small electrical current is directed into the water, temporarily stunning any fish in the immediate area. They rose to the surface, allowing us to take a census and measure and weigh some of them. Then the fish were returned to the water unharmed.

That, at least, was the way things should have gone in theory, but to a full-grown snakehead, this electric pulse was nothing but an annoyance. We turned on the juice and, instantly, a three-foot monster jumped out of the water over our heads and into the boat. "Kill that f***ing fish," cried out my boss, Melissa, who until that moment had been one of the most soft-spoken women I'd ever known. You see, since the snakehead was an invasive species, she had no problem with our getting rid of it before it could prey on more native fish. The DEC has tried to enlist the help of anglers in getting rid of this illegal alien. If you catch a snakehead you are supposed to kill it and take it to the DEC.

Back to the story: I jumped on the fish and actually tackled it and wrestled it for a few minutes before I could gain control of it and put it in the cooler. The damned fish would not die . . . snakehead live out of water with something that resembles a pair of lungs. The thing just continued thrashing around and smashing the lid of the cooler. I had to finally sit on the cooler so the bugger could not get out!

Since then I have taken it as my environmental duty to capture and cook snakehead as often as I can. So far, the snakehead are winning because I haven't had much luck, but I'll keep trying because I find them delicious. In addition to going for snakehead with rod and reel, bow hunting for them is a new hot sport. Try it. It works, it's exciting. Do it at night and you'll end up with a mess of snakehead in your boat. Big ones!

Angry SNAKEHEAD
WITH THAI CURRY VEGETABLES

I curl the fish in the pot when I fry it. It looks fierce. Served in a wide soup bowl, it looks like a snakehead swimming in its own lake. But you'll need a medium- to small-size snakehead for this effect unless you want to serve your soup in a tub.

Soup

¼ cup vegetable oil

3 garlic cloves, minced

3 medium shallots, minced

1 Thai chile, minced

2-inch piece of fresh ginger, peeled and thinly sliced

2 tablespoons Thai red curry paste

1 tablespoon, packed, palm or light brown sugar

2 tablespoons tamarind purée

¼ cup fish sauce

3 tablespoons fresh lime juice

2 cups 1-inch cauliflower florets

1 cup green beans, preferably long beans, cut into 1-inch lengths

Salt and freshly ground black pepper

8 baby bok choy, rinsed well

8 Chinese broccoli stems, trimmed

Fish

Vegetable oil, for deep frying

1 (3-pound) snakefish or pike, gutted and scaled, back fin cut out

Salt and freshly ground black pepper

½ cup rice flour

½ cup cornstarch

SERVES 4

1. To prepare the soup: In a large pot, heat the oil. Add the garlic, shallots, Thai chile, and ginger and cook over medium-low heat until fragrant and golden, about 5 minutes. Add the curry paste and palm sugar and cook over medium heat, stirring, until fragrant, about 2 minutes. Add the tamarind puree, fish sauce, lime juice, and 1½ cups water and bring to a boil, stirring well. Add the cauliflower and green beans and simmer over medium heat until just tender, about 4 minutes. Season with salt and a generous amount of pepper, cover, and remove from the heat.

2. To prepare the fish: Use a very large heavy, deep skillet or pot at least 16 inches wide (to hold the whole fish). If necessary, cut the head off the fish so it will fit. Add enough vegetable oil to the skillet to reach about 1½ inches up the sides. Heat the oil to 375°F. Make 2 slashes on each side of the fish, cutting only halfway through. Season the fish inside and out with salt and pepper.

3. Combine the rice flour and cornstarch on a large platter and season lightly with salt and pepper. Dredge the fish in the flour mixture to coat thoroughly, shaking off excess. Fry the fish in the hot oil until golden brown and crisp on the bottom, about 7 minutes. Carefully turn the fish and fry for about 5 minutes longer, until just cooked through.

4. Meanwhile, line a rimmed baking sheet with paper towels and have a clean platter ready. Reheat the vegetable soup, add the bok choy and Chinese broccoli, and simmer for 1½ to 2 minutes, until they are just crisp. With 2 sets of tongs, gently lift the fish from the oil and transfer to the paper towels to drain. Drain on the paper towels quickly so the fish stays crisp, then transfer to the platter.

5. Serve the soup in shallow bowls and, at the table, lift the meat from both sides of the fish with 2 forks to add to the soup.

SNAKEHEAD CHIMICHURRI TACOS

I owe this recipe to Chad Wells, a badass chef and extreme fisherman whom I met at Alewife in Baltimore. He has a whitewater kayak outfitted for fishing, and he is one of those crazy guys who enjoys fishing with a weapons-grade compound bow, like what hunters use for deer or elk. On the day he took me out for snakehead with rod and reel we were skunked—as in nada, nugatory, strikeout. He tried to make it up to me by inviting me and another buddy (Mike Louie) to a snakehead derby, where everyone but us had a compound bow! We were also missing the camo outfits and the face paint. Mike and I rolled snake eyes for snakehead, as in we caught zero. That night, Chad, who was more successful, whipped up these tacos.

For those of you unfamiliar with chimichurri, it is a fresh Argentine sauce of olive oil, salt, parsley, garlic, chiles, and oregano usually used on steak. I like it on fish and even mashed potatoes.

4 garlic cloves, minced

⅓ cup olive oil

⅓ cup chopped fresh flat-leaf parsley

2 tablespoons white vinegar

1½ teaspoons dried oregano

½ teaspoon chile flakes

Salt and freshly ground black pepper

1¼ pounds skinned snakefish or catfish fillet, cut crosswise into 1-inch-thick slices

Savoy Cabbage Slaw with Chipotle (page 237)

Grilled Corn Salsa (page 242)

Eight to ten 6-inch corn tortillas, oiled and grilled, for serving

SERVES 4

1 In a small bowl, make the chimichurri by combining the garlic, olive oil, parsley, vinegar, oregano, and chile flakes, and season with salt and pepper. Put the sliced fish in a large bowl and pour over half the chimichurri (set aside the other half). Toss well to completely coat the fish. Cover, refrigerate, and marinate for up to 2 hours.

2 Take the slaw and salsa out of the refrigerator. Heat a large skillet. Add half the marinated fish and cook over high heat until browned and cooked, about 2 minutes per side. Adjust the heat to medium-high as needed. Repeat with the remaining fish.

3 Serve the fish with the slaw, salsa, reserved chimichurri, and grilled tortillas.

The chimichurri can be refrigerated for up to 4 days.

For those of you unfamiliar with chimichurri, it is a fresh Argentine sauce of olive oil, salt, parsley, garlic, chiles, and oregano usually used on steak. I like it on fish and even mashed potatoes.

SNAPPER

What a fun name for a fish. It's like a dog named Spike or a cat named Boots; you just can't help liking something named snapper. In fact, these fish are so well liked and delicious that fishing pressure has endangered many of the most popular snappers in U.S. waters. Check out the most local and up-to-date sustainable seafood information you can find to see what they say about snapper sustainability.

Snappers are part of a large family of fish found in warm waters all over the globe. There are more than sixty species, but they all have two things in common: delicious mild, flaky flesh, and nasty sharp teeth. Hence the name *snapper*. I haven't had a lot of experience fishing for snappers (they rarely make it as far north as my home waters), but I did film an episode of *Hook, Line & Dinner* in Key West featuring mutton snapper, which is still quite plentiful. They are quick little guys. If you don't hook 'em right away and keep them out of the rocks, they're going to break off.

When I was hooking one, my guide frantically told me I had thirty seconds to whip this fish or he would take me into the rocks and cut me off. Not wanting to lose my fish, I began reeling like a maniac, convinced it was a big fish. We were fishing in deep water so I was fighting both the fish and the weight of the water. I was wearing a standing harness, and every time the fish lunged, I was pulled up on my tiptoes and almost over the side. That day, I got a real big one plus a smaller one, and I worked up a real sweat doing so. Getting my catch to the restaurant proved kind of iffy.

On my way to meet the chef, Doug Shook, at the restaurant, Louie's Backyard, we decided to film the fish as I transported them via motorcycle. I placed a little handheld camera on the back of my bike and turned it to face the fish, so the camera could film the fish on the seat of the bike as I drove off. Cool idea, right? When I arrived at the restaurant I discovered that the bigger of the two fish, the one I had placed on the bottom, had disappeared en route. We were supposed to do a cooking demo, so everyone was really angry at me for suggesting the motorcycle delivery. With only one fish to work with, we had to nail the demo perfectly on the first take. Hoping we might find the other fish, we retraced my route. But there was no sign of the fugitive snapper. Later on, we reviewed the camera footage to see what had happened, and in the last edit, we saw it: a shot of the snapper falling off my bike and landing in the road, clear as day, with me driving off without a clue! I'm sure some passing raccoon was glad to come across a free meal.

Surfer's SNAPPER CHOWDER

2 tablespoons vegetable oil

1 pound red-skinned potatoes, scrubbed and cut into ¾-inch cubes

Salt and freshly ground black pepper

½ pound sliced bacon

2 large leeks, white and pale green parts only, thinly sliced

1 garlic clove, minced

½ teaspoon ground coriander

Pinch of cayenne pepper

½ cup dry white wine, such as pinot grigio

2 cups vegetable stock

1 teaspoon finely grated orange zest

½ cup fresh orange juice

1 (14.5-ounce) can diced tomatoes

2 tablespoons unsalted butter

2 tablespoons fresh lime juice

2 tablespoons Asian fish sauce

1 large jalapeño, roasted, seeded, and minced

1 pound snapper fillet, skinned, cut into 1-inch pieces

2 tablespoons chopped fresh flat-leaf parsley

Garlic salt

4 small watermelon halves, scooped out, for serving

SERVES 4

The word *chowder* always brings to mind images of chilly days and a hearty restorative meal in a bowl. But when living on a Caribbean island, you want something with lots of flavor that fills you up and comes together quickly. This snapper chowder was my answer. Using non-standard chowder ingredients, such as orange juice and Asian fish sauce, it is substantial in a chowdery way, but with light tropical notes. I first made it when I was living on a boat in St. John, in the Virgin Islands. One day I returned home from surfing to find my boat was gone and I was reduced to living on the beach with a surfboard, a makeshift sleeping bag, and a camp stove. It was primitive, but I made a stripped down version of this recipe with basically no equipment and it is now one of my favorite meals when I am in the islands and want something to eat when I am bone-tired from surfing or fishing. By the way, I got the boat back. Long story. Lots of hassles. This chowder is more memorable than that boat.

1   In a large cast-iron skillet, heat the vegetable oil. Add the potatoes, turn to coat with the oil, and season with salt and pepper. Cook over medium heat until browned on the bottom, about 4 minutes. Turn the potatoes and cook for about 5 minutes longer, until crisp all over and just tender.

2   Meanwhile, in a large pot, cook the bacon over medium heat until crisp, about 5 minutes. Drain the bacon on paper towels and crumble coarsely. Pour off all but 3 tablespoons of the bacon fat and add the leeks. Season with salt and pepper and cook over medium heat, stirring a few times, until softened, about 5 minutes. Add the potatoes and stir well. Add the garlic, coriander, and cayenne and cook, stirring, until fragrant, about 1 minute. Add the wine and simmer over medium-high heat for 1 minute. Add the stock, orange zest and juice, the tomatoes, and butter and bring to a boil. Simmer over low heat for 5 minutes. Stir in the lime juice, fish sauce, and roasted jalapeño and simmer for 3 minutes.

3   Season the snapper pieces with salt and pepper and add to the chowder with the parsley. Simmer until the fish starts to flake, about 3 minutes. Season the chowder with garlic salt and ladle into the watermelon bowls. Garnish with the crumbled bacon and serve.

Pan-Fried CUBAN SNAPPER
WITH CUBAN GARLIC & SOUR-ORANGE SAUCE

Simply pan-fried until crisp, these smaller snappers are served with a classic Cuban sauce of mashed, fried garlic that simmers in sour-orange juice. Figure a 1¼-pound snapper for two people. The smaller size is more manageable for pan-frying—any larger and you may want the larger area of a grill. Sour oranges are used all over Mexico and the Caribbean. I love 'em because you get this floral, citrusy flavor but not the candy sweetness of orange juice.

8 medium garlic cloves, peeled and chopped a few times

½ teaspoon coarsely cracked black pepper

⅓ cup olive oil

¼ teaspoon chile flakes

4 (3-inch-long) orange zest strips

½ cup fresh sour-orange juice or ½ cup fresh orange juice with 3 tablespoons fresh lime juice

Salt and freshly ground black pepper

Vegetable oil, for frying

2 (1- to 1¼-pound) whole snappers, gutted, scaled, and gilled

½ cup chopped fresh cilantro

SERVES 4

1 With a mortar and pestle, smash the garlic and black pepper together to make a coarse paste. In a medium saucepan, heat the olive oil over medium heat. Add the garlic paste, chile flakes, and orange zest strips and cook over low heat, stirring a few times, until the garlic is golden and the oil richly flavored, about 7 minutes. Take the pan off the heat a few times, if necessary, to keep the garlic from getting too dark while it develops flavor. Add the sour-orange juice and simmer for 1 minute. Remove from the heat and season with salt.

2 In each of two 14-inch-wide skillets, heat ¼ inch of oil until shimmering. Make 2 slashes in each side of the fish almost to the bone. Pat the fish completely dry with paper towels and season inside and out with salt and pepper. Use splatter screens and fry the fish over medium-high heat without disturbing until browned and crisp, about 6 minutes per side. Transfer the fish to 1 large or 2 smaller platters. With 2 forks, lift the meat from the bones and place on plates. Stir the cilantro into the garlic and sour-orange sauce and pass at the table.

STRIPED BASS

If there is a king of game fish in the Northeast, it is the striper. As I write this, I remember a magical, psychedelic striper experience I had with my father when I was a young boy. At night my dad and I would fish on a jetty. It was a still summer night, so quiet that you could hear the stripers working their way through the baitfish around the jetty. Suddenly, bam! A ball made up of a hundred brilliant colors tore across the sky, seeming to head straight for us before passing overhead and beyond the horizon. I looked up at my dad to see if he had anything to say about it, anything reassuring, or to see if he even saw it, but we both just sat there, stunned at what must have been the last moments of a meteorite. It was the most surreal moment of my life.

When stripers blitz the shore, chasing baitfish, it is sheer mayhem. They are so crazed with bloodlust that they will sometimes beach themselves and you can actually pick them up with your hands. White-fleshed, with beautiful pinstripes on the sides, ranging from two to fifty pounds, they are the champs of my game-fishing world.

I have earned my stripes with these guys. I have climbed barbed wire to fish illegal spots and almost been arrested. I have been fined for trespassing in New York City trying to get to a secret spot. In Montauk, I have literally fished with the fish. It's a technique called skitching invented by Paul Melnyk. As a surf fisherman, he finally could no longer take watching pods of frenzied feeding fish just out of casting range. Instead of buying or renting a boat, he hit upon the idea of putting on fins and swimming into the middle of the mass of boiling fish! Not a good idea for about five hundred reasons. One, Montauk is notoriously sharky, as in the biggest Great White ever caught on rod and reel was landed there. And if you are successful you have dead fish (i.e., fresh shark bait) tied to your belt and you are out in deep, dark shark water. Two, during the autumn run there are frenzied chomping fish for as far as the eye can see, among them acres of bluefish—which will chomp your finger or something even more important right off! Long story short, I tried it, I liked it, I caught fish; but I don't plan to make a habit of skitching.

Here's a different kind of chowder, based on, of all things, broccoli rabe!

STRIPED BASS CHOWDER
WITH BROCCOLI RABE PESTO

Pesto and florets

1¼ pounds broccoli rabe, lower stems cut off

¼ cup toasted pine nuts

1 garlic clove, minced

1½ tablespoons capers, drained and chopped

1½ teaspoons finely grated lemon zest

¼ cup grated Parmesan

½ cup plus 1 tablespoon olive oil

Salt and freshly ground black pepper

Chowder

2 tablespoons olive oil

2 medium leeks, white and pale green parts, thinly sliced

Pinch of cayenne pepper

1 cup canned stewed tomatoes, chopped

½ pound Yukon Gold potatoes, peeled and sliced ¼ inch thick

3 cups Fish Stock (page 113) or clam juice

¼ cup light cream

1 pound striped bass fillet, skinned and cut into 1½-inch pieces

SERVES 4 TO 6

Here's a different kind of chowder, based on, of all things, broccoli rabe! I love all the vegetables in the broccoli family (which includes cauliflower and broccoli rabe), though many people think of them as "good-for-you," but not necessarily a lot of fun. However, make it into a pesto and you've got fun. Everyone likes pesto. My friends always enjoy stirring it into their chowder at the table. It makes for a nice, light chowder, with a crisp finish.

1. To prepare the pesto and florets: In a large pot of boiling water, cook the broccoli rabe until tender, about 2 minutes. Drain and cool. Cut off all the florets and reserve. Chop the stems and leaves and transfer to a food processor. Add the pine nuts, garlic, capers, and lemon zest and process to coarsely chop. Add the cheese and all the olive oil and puree. Season with salt and pepper.

2. To prepare the chowder: In a large pot, heat the olive oil. Add the leeks and cook over medium-low heat, stirring a few times, until softened, about 7 minutes. Add the cayenne and cook for about 20 seconds. Add the tomatoes, potatoes, stock, and 1 cup water and bring to a boil. Partially cover and simmer over medium-low heat until the potatoes are tender, about 10 minutes. Add the cream and striped bass and simmer until the fish is just cooked, about 3 minutes. Remove from the heat and add the reserved broccoli rabe florets.

3. Ladle the chowder into bowls and pass the pesto at the table to stir in.

The broccoli rabe pesto and blanched florets can be refrigerated, separately, overnight. Bring to room temperature before using.

SALSA STRIPER in FOIL
WITH CARAMELIZED ENDIVES

Think of this method as making a stew without a stew pot. Wrapping fish fillets in foil and letting them roast on the grill to form an aromatic stew is a good method when you are camping or have limited cooking utensils. The individual foil packets form makeshift bowls that each person can eat from. Even better, there are no plates to wash afterward. The fun part is layering in the flavors and garnishes, such as chopped or thinly sliced vegetables, wine, olive oil, and salsa, all of which meld into a delicious recipe. A good amount of butter goes in the bottom of the packet so the endives become beautifully caramelized.

Hot Summer Salsa (page 236)

8 tablespoons (1 stick) unsalted butter

4 Belgian endives, cored and sliced crosswise ½ inch thick

Salt

4 (½-pound) striped bass fillets, skinned

2 tablespoons olive oil

½ cup dry white wine

SERVES 4

1   Cover and refrigerate the salsa for 30 minutes.

2   Light a grill. Cut out 8 sheets of heavy-duty foil, about 20 inches long and 12 to 14 inches wide. Make 4 double layers and place 2 tablespoons of butter in the center of each. Put 1 sliced endive over the butter, spreading it out a little, and season with salt. Season the bass fillets with salt and put a fillet over each endive. Bring up the sides of the foil and drizzle each fillet with ½ tablespoon of olive oil. Drizzle 2 tablespoons of wine over each fillet and spoon over ¼ cup of salsa along with 2 tablespoons of the tomato juices from the salsa. Fold up the packages tightly but leave space around the fish for steam to expand.

3   Grill the packages over a hot fire until sizzling inside and the packages start to expand, about 17 minutes. Turn the packages around halfway through cooking.

4   Let the packages rest for about 5 minutes. Eat out of the packages or transfer to bowls to serve.

Salt-Baked BIG STRIPER

This is a recipe learned from the great master of fire cooking, Argentina's Francis Mall-mann. If you are tired of turkey and prime rib at holiday dinners, here's a substitute that gives up nothing in the dramatic-impression department. Francis makes his by building two roaring fires on huge metal plates and then sandwiching the salt-crusted bass between the fire above and the fire below. Nothing so daunting is required here, where his method is adapted for a home oven. Just make sure to spread lots of paper under the pans when you pack the salt, otherwise you will have a messy kitchen. Likewise, put some aluminum foil under the baking tray in the oven. The fresh salsa is also quite nice on the potatoes and sweet potatoes that cook with the fish.

Fish

8 medium carrots, scrubbed

5 (3-pound) boxes kosher salt

1 (8-pound) striped bass, gutted but unscaled

4 medium Idaho potatoes, skin scrubbed

4 medium sweet potatoes, skin scrubbed

Sauce

2 cups olive oil

1 cup chopped fresh flat-leaf parsley

½ cup chopped garlic

½ cup fresh oregano leaves

Zest of 2 lemons, minced

Flaky sea salt, to taste

Freshly ground black pepper, to taste

SERVES 8

The fresh salsa is also quite nice on the potatoes and sweet potatoes that cook with the fish.

1 To prepare the fish: Preheat the oven to 500°F. Clean the sink and place a stopper in the drain. Place the carrots in a single layer on a sheet of foil and wrap tightly to make a sealed bundle.

2 Lay newspaper next to the sink and on top of the paper place a rimmed baking sheet large enough to fit the fish. There should be about 1 foot of paper on all sides of the sheet pan to catch any overflow of salt. Pour 1 box of salt into the stoppered sink. Mix the salt and 8 cups of water by hand. It should have the consistency of wet spring snow. Add 1 more box of salt and moisten with more water to the consistency called for. Fill the bottom of the sheet pan with the salt mixture and tamp down so you have about 1 inch of compacted salt. Lay the fish on top of the salt.

3 Lay the foil-wrapped carrots on the salt and surround the fish with the potatoes and sweet potatoes. No foil is needed for the potatoes and sweet potatoes, since the skin protects their flesh while roasting. Make another batch of wet salt using 2 more boxes of salt and water as needed. Cover the fish and vegetables with more moist salt, as you would if you were covering someone at the beach in sand. Tamp down the salt firmly. It should cover the ingredients with a layer about 1 inch thick. You may need to use the last box of salt here to make more wet salt. Stick a meat thermometer (not instant-read) through the salt and into the fish.

4 Very carefully place the baking sheet in the lower third of the oven. Depending on the size of the fish, you may need two people to do this. Bake until a meat thermometer reaches 150°F, which should be after approximately 55 minutes. Let the thermometer be your guide.

5 Meanwhile, prepare the sauce: In a medium bowl, combine the olive oil, parsley, garlic, oregano, and lemon zest and season with the sea salt and pepper.

6 Remove the salt-covered fish and pan from the oven and let rest for 20 minutes. Again, you may need two people to remove a larger fish.

7 Tap the salt crust with a hammer or wooden mallet until it cracks. It will come off in big chunks. Use oven mitts or a dish towel to handle the hot salt. Discard the salt in the trash, or toss it into the sink and run water on it. Remove and reserve the vegetables. With a pastry brush, remove the remaining salt from the fish, and, using a thin-bladed knife, lift off and discard the fish skin.

8 To serve, use 2 large spoons to lift individual servings of fish from the backbone and transfer to plates. Place a carrot, half a potato, and half a sweet potato on each plate. Garnish with the sauce and serve.

SWORD-FISH

Fishing for swordfish really means battling: honestly, like going to war. It is one of the great trophy fish, true big game. Swordfish follow the Gulf Stream up the East Coast, so you can catch them anywhere from Mexico to New England. I battled one for three arduous hours once—he was fifteen hundred feet beneath me in the water, and I was exhausted and drenched in sweat, and just when I didn't think I had one crank left in me, the fish spotted our boat. It was as if he hadn't done one ounce of pulling because he rocketed down to the bottom, to the depths, and my line whirled down with him. I knew there was nothing I could do—I just had to let him go and start reeling in once again after he had pulled out my line all the way into the backing. I was sure this fish weighed a couple hundred pounds, but when I finally pulled him out of the water, he was not huge; in fact, he was relatively small for a swordfish. It's common for a swordfish to feel huge and come up short or feel short and come up a monster. Although this guy was legal size, I decided to give him some more years to grow up and fight other fishermen, so I let him go.

I love eating swordfish. It has a distinctive texture and meatiness, and tastes nothing like any other fish. When cooked properly its color, texture, and juiciness remind me of a beautiful succulent Berkshire pork chop. It took me years and years to learn how to cook swordfish properly. Like most salmon you've likely had growing up, the swordfish I had was always overcooked. But I've learned it's a great indicating fish—by that I mean it "tells you when it's done" because the spirals in its flesh start to open up as you cook, and without having to cut into the fish, you can push your finger into the middle of the spiral. If your finger goes in easily, that's when you know the fish is done. Neat trick. No more dried-out swordfish.

Tamarind-Glazed SWORDFISH
WITH HOT AND SOUR SOUP

The glazed swordfish is terrific just on its own. But rich and dense swordfish can take strong flavors, so a hot and sour soup is a great base for it. Cutting the swordfish into chunks makes the cooking go fast and the tamarind and brown butter glaze is intensely good. After breaking down a sword you will have a lot of trimmings left over. These are great for soup. You don't necessarily have to catch a sword to do this. Many fish markets will be happy to sell you the trimmings quite inexpensively.

Soup

1 tablespoon unsalted butter

1 large shallot, thinly sliced

1 garlic clove, minced

½ teaspoon chile flakes

4 thin peeled fresh ginger slices, about ⅛ inch thick

3 lime zest strips, about ½ inch wide

2 large plum tomatoes, finely chopped

2 tablespoons soy sauce or tamari

1 lemongrass stalk, lower third, cut into 1-inch lengths and smashed

2½ tablespoons tamarind puree

1 cup unsweetened coconut water

¼ cup clam juice

¼ pound thin green beans or long beans, cut into ½-inch lengths

2 ears corn, kernels cut from the cobs

¼ cup rich coconut milk

Salt and freshly ground black pepper

Lime wedges, for serving

Swordfish

3 tablespoons unsalted butter

1½ pounds swordfish, skinned and cut into 1-inch cubes

Salt

1 tablespoon plus 2 teaspoons tamarind puree

1 tablespoon plus 2 teaspoons ketchup

Pinch of chile flakes

SERVES 4

To make the soup: In a large pot, melt the butter. Add the shallot and garlic, cover, and cook over medium-low heat, stirring a few times, until soft and starting to brown, about 6 minutes. Add the chile flakes, ginger, and lime zest strips, cover, and cook for 2 minutes. Add the tomatoes and cook over medium heat until they cook down to a sauce, about 4 minutes. Add the soy sauce and cook until richly flavored, about 2 minutes. Add the lemongrass, tamarind puree, coconut water, and clam juice and bring to a boil. Add the green beans and corn, cover, and simmer over low heat until the beans are tender, about 5 minutes. Stir in the coconut milk and season with salt and pepper.

2 To make the swordfish: In a large nonstick skillet, melt the butter over medium-high heat. When the foaming stops, add the swordfish in an even layer and season lightly with salt. Cook until browned on the bottom, about 2 minutes. Shake the skillet and brown the swordfish cubes on the other sides, cooking another minute or so, until the swordfish is just cooked. When lightly pressed, you should feel the grain of the fish start to separate. Add the tamarind, ketchup, and chile flakes and stir well to coat the swordfish with the glaze. Working quickly, add 1 or 2 tablespoons of water (just enough to make a thick sauce) and remove the skillet from the heat. Swirl the swordfish in the sauce to coat well, putting back on the heat briefly if necessary to keep hot.

3 Ladle the soup into shallow bowls. Scrape the swordfish and sauce into each portion of soup and serve with lime wedges.

You don't necessarily have to catch a sword to do this. Many fish markets will be happy to sell you the trimmings quite inexpensively.

GRILLED SWORDFISH
WITH HERBED BEURRE BLANC

Everyday herbs like chives, parsley, and basil are great with fish, but so are other less common ones. Sage leaves, when fried and crisp, hit the spot and add such a wonderful texture and flavor. Your guests will be blown away. Beurre blanc is a simple French sauce made with vinegar (or white wine), shallots, and chilled butter slowly stirred in so the sauce emulsifies and becomes a creamy, tangy, buttery liquid that goes with any white-fleshed fish. This is a molto simple way to do swordfish . . . but in my opinion, there's none better.

1 tablespoon olive oil, plus more for the fish

16 fresh sage leaves

Salt and freshly ground black pepper

1 large shallot, minced

¼ cup dry white wine

3 tablespoons white wine vinegar

1 stick unsalted butter, cut into 8 tablespoons, chilled

4 (6- to 8-ounce) swordfish fillets, about 1 inch thick

2 tablespoons minced fresh chives

1 teaspoon chopped fresh tarragon

SERVES 4

1 In a medium skillet, heat the olive oil. Add the sage leaves and cook over medium-high heat until the leaves are crisp, about 1 minute per side. Tilt the skillet and with a fork, transfer the sage leaves to a plate. Season lightly with salt and pepper.

2 In a small skillet, combine the shallot, wine, and vinegar and boil over high heat until the liquid is reduced to 1 tablespoon, about 3 minutes. Remove the skillet from the heat for about 1 minute to cool it down a little, then reduce the heat to low and put the skillet back on the burner. Whisk in the butter, only 1 tablespoon at a time, adding the next tablespoon when the previous one is almost incorporated. Whisk the sauce constantly to keep a smooth and emulsified texture, and take the skillet off the burner often to make sure the butter doesn't melt and get oily. You want just enough heat to incorporate the butter. When all the butter has been blended in, remove from the heat and set aside.

3 Light a grill. Drizzle the swordfish with olive oil and season with salt and pepper. Grill over a hot fire until nicely charred and slightly underdone in the center, about 3 minutes per side. Press the swordfish with your fingers; you should feel the grain of the fish start to separate. Put the swordfish on a platter and let rest for a few minutes.

4 Add the chives and tarragon to the beurre blanc and put the skillet over medium heat while whisking constantly, taking the skillet off the heat once or twice. Whisk until the sauce is warm to the touch, silky, and pourable, about 1 minute. Remove from the heat and season with salt and pepper.

5 Pour the beurre blanc over the swordfish. Garnish with the crisp sage leaves and serve.

TROUT

For many anglers, trout are the peak of the sport. Sometimes I feel that way, especially when I fish for them with a fly rod, which is how I fished when I lived in Vermont. Watching rising trout sip at mayflies as they drift down a pretty stream is both beautiful and exciting. We have three types of what are commonly thought of as trout in the United States. There is the brook trout, native to the cool rivers and streams of the East. There is the colorful and acrobatic rainbow trout, originally a Western species. Lately scientists have decided that neither of these fish is a true trout, but ask any fisherman and you will find there are plenty of trout-loving loyalists who include rainbows and brookies in the world of troutdom. Finally, there is a true trout, the brown trout, brought here from Europe in the nineteenth century. Basically all have the same size and shape, thrive in the same waters, and eat the same foods, so when you cook them you'd be hard-pressed to tell the difference.

I have a funny relationship with trout. Like most fly fishermen I agree we should not be harvesting too many, if any, out of our lakes and rivers. The trout is what's known as a top predator. Just as there are fewer lions than impala, there are far fewer trout than forage fish, so it doesn't take much to deplete a trout fishery. Still, a wild trout every now and then reminds us how great these fish are and to value them. And anyway, if I chase one freaking trout down a stream and almost drown myself in the process, I want to keep it. I am talking about wild fish here. Hatchery-raised trout are a different story. I never mind taking a few of those for the pan. How do you know if a fish is hatchery-raised or wild? Usually there is a sign or some indication on a fishing map or the web. Anyone in a fly shop should know.

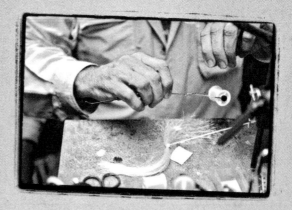

Chilled TROUT SOUP
WITH AVOCADO & RADISHES

I once hosted a confab in Monterey, California, where chefs got together to trade ideas about sustainable seafood. While walking through the test kitchen I was introduced to Barton Seaver. He is a great chef and a passionate spokesman for preserving our wild fisheries. I love his cookbook *For Cod and Country*, and I rattled off four recipes on the spot that I cook all the time. I think I must have seemed a little starstruck. This is one of those recipes. It really emphasizes the delicacy of trout. The fresh vegetables and lime juice combine for unusual lightness in a chowder.

2 medium-size ripe avocados, peeled, pitted, and diced

3 tablespoons fresh lime juice

1 cup clam juice

2 tablespoons chopped fresh dill and/or cilantro

Salt and freshly ground black pepper

4 red radishes with greens, radishes thinly sliced

Olive oil

½ pound smoked trout fillet, skinned, broken up

Crème fraîche

SERVES 4 TO 6

1 In a blender, combine the avocados, lime juice, clam juice, 1 cup of water, and the herbs and puree. Transfer to a large glass bowl and season with salt and pepper. Refrigerate until chilled.

2 In a small pot of boiling water, cook the radish greens for about 1 minute. Drain, squeeze out some of the water, and chop. In a small skillet, warm a little olive oil. Add the radish greens and cook over moderately high heat, stirring, until hot. Season with salt and pepper.

3 Check the thickness of the soup. If it's too thick, add a few tablespoons of water. Ladle the soup into bowls. Place the radishes and greens, trout pieces, and some crème fraîche on top and serve.

Freshly Caught POACHED BLUE TROUT

Read any of the French fish cookery books that came out in English from the late 1940s through the 1960s and you will find this recipe. It's nothing more than a poached whole trout, but something about the vinegar in the broth turns the skin of a just-caught trout a deep blue. It looks unbelievably cool, kind of magical; but, then, trout have inhabited the imagination of anglers since the dawn of fishing. This recipe is for trout cooked just after they are caught. Otherwise the fish will actually taste the same, but they won't turn blue!

1 quart Fish Stock (page 113), though water will do if that's all you have

½ cup white wine vinegar

2 live trout, about ¾ to 1 pound each

SERVES 2

1 Bring the stock and vinegar to a boil over high heat in a long, narrow poaching pan (or any pan that holds the whole fish, if no poaching pan is available). Kill the live trout with a sharp blow to the head. Immediately gut the fish and plunge the trout into the boiling stock; let it return to a boil.

2 Remove the pan from the heat and cover for 5 to 8 minutes. Remove the fish by lifting it out of the poaching rack (or by using a pair of slotted spatulas) and serve.

HASH BROWN TROUT CAKES
WITH SPINACH & POTATO

There is nothing like a streamside lunch or breakfast with a fresh-caught fish. This is another recipe I learned from the great Francis Mallmann (see page 208). It is an easy one-skillet meal cooked over a campfire or a stove. I made this in Craig, Montana, along the Missouri River. It's my idea of a perfect fisherman's town: an amazing river, a couple of fly shops, a few places to stay, a bar that makes great late-night burgers, and a breakfast place that opens early.

2 pounds Idaho potatoes

1 small onion, thinly sliced

Salt and freshly ground black pepper

4 to 5 tablespoons unsalted butter

¼ to ⅓ cup vegetable oil

1¼ pounds trout fillets, skinned, cut into 4 pieces

8 large spinach leaves, stemmed

SERVES 4

1　Put the potatoes in a large saucepan, cover with water, and bring to a boil. Cook over medium-high heat for 15 minutes, or until they start to soften on the outside. Drain, cool, and peel the potatoes. Shred the potatoes on a box grater into a large bowl. Add the onion and salt and pepper and toss well.

2　In a large cast-iron skillet, melt 2 tablespoons of the butter in 2 tablespoons of the oil. When hot, add half the potatoes and press in an even layer. Season the trout with salt and pepper and place over the potatoes, equally spaced apart. Place 2 spinach leaves over each piece of trout and cover with the remaining potatoes. Cook over medium-low heat, pressing a few times, until crisp and browned on the bottom, about 20 minutes.

3　With a spatula, cut in between the trout to make 4 portions. Flip the portions and add 2 tablespoons of the butter and 2 tablespoons of the oil to the skillet. Press and cook for about 10 minutes longer, adding more butter and oil as needed, to get a good crust.

4　Using the spatula, scrape the portions from the bottom of the skillet. Transfer to plates and serve.

WALLEYE

Anyone who has fished in the Midwest has probably heard someone say words much like the following: "You can have your trout and you can have your bass, but for my money, the walleye is the best eatin' fish there is . . . bar none!" Don't forget the "bar none" part; they really lean on that. Once upon a time, walleye were a big commercial fishery in the United States. I've seen late-nineteenth-century pictures of barges in Sandusky, Ohio, on the Sandusky River, piled high with walleye. Overfishing put an end to commercial harvesting. That's usually the case with freshwater fisheries: It's easy for a fishing fleet to degrade it very quickly. Thankfully, with regulation, walleye stocks have been recovering and recreational fishermen can still enjoy the best eatin' fish there is.

In the same way that the opening of dove season is practically a national holiday in the South, or deer season in Pennsylvania, Minnesotans celebrate the departure of winter with a massive "gone fishin'" exodus on the opening day of walleye season. With a population of fewer than five million people, it's really impressive that there are a million boats being trailered to Minnesota's lakes and rivers on that day. Right along with their Vikings and Twins, Minnesotans love Opening Day.

In Minnesota, it can still be mighty chilly early in the morning in May and plenty of fishermen start out in their snowmobile suits. Although it is not written into the Minnesota constitution, the governor is always out there at first light, and the progress of his fishing trip is reported with the gusto that Punxsutawney Phil gets on Groundhog Day (and with about as much respect). He rarely, if ever, lands the first walleye of the season. If you have an old fish cookbook, you may see the words *walleyed pike*. Some modern menus still use this term, too. Don't be misled. It's a walleye, not a pike.

WALLEYE CHOWDER
WITH POTATOES & TABASCO OIL

This started out as a fishless chowder that I had once in Michigan. I liked the body and creaminess that pureed potatoes gave it. After catching a few walleye one afternoon, I realized that this chowder didn't have to be fishless any longer. Walleye is very mild in taste but the chowder gets a lot of zip from the Tabasco.

1 pound sliced bacon, cut crosswise into ¼-inch-thick sticks

1 leek, white and light green parts, thinly sliced

1 medium onion, thinly sliced

4 large Idaho potatoes (2¼ pounds), peeled and cut into 1-inch dice

1 quart heavy cream

1½ cups whole milk

Salt and freshly ground black pepper

½ cup vegetable oil

¼ cup Tabasco

1½ pounds walleye fillet, skinned and cut into 1-inch pieces

½ cup minced fresh chives, for garnish

SERVES 8

1 In a large heavy pot, combine the bacon and 2 tablespoons water. Cook over medium heat, stirring a few times, until the water evaporates and the bacon crisps, about 15 minutes. With a slotted spoon, drain the bacon on paper towels, leaving ¼ cup of the fat in the pan. Add the leek and onion and cook, partially covered, until translucent, about 10 minutes. Add the potatoes, cream, and milk, stir well, and season lightly with salt and pepper. Simmer over low heat, partially covered, until the potatoes are soft, about 30 minutes. With an immersion blender or potato masher, mash the potatoes to the consistency you like.

2 Meanwhile, in a small saucepan combine the oil and Tabasco and simmer over low heat, undisturbed, until bright red, about 7 minutes. Remove from the heat and let stand for a few minutes to settle. Pour through a fine strainer into a small bowl, stopping before you reach the solids at the bottom. Let cool.

3 Season the walleye pieces with salt and pepper and add to the soup. Simmer over medium-low heat, stirring a few times, until the fish is cooked through, about 5 minutes. Season the soup with salt and pepper and ladle into bowls. Garnish with the bacon and chives. Drizzle with some Tabasco oil and serve.

The soup, without the fish, can be refrigerated for up to 2 days. Add the fish to the soup after reheating and just before serving.

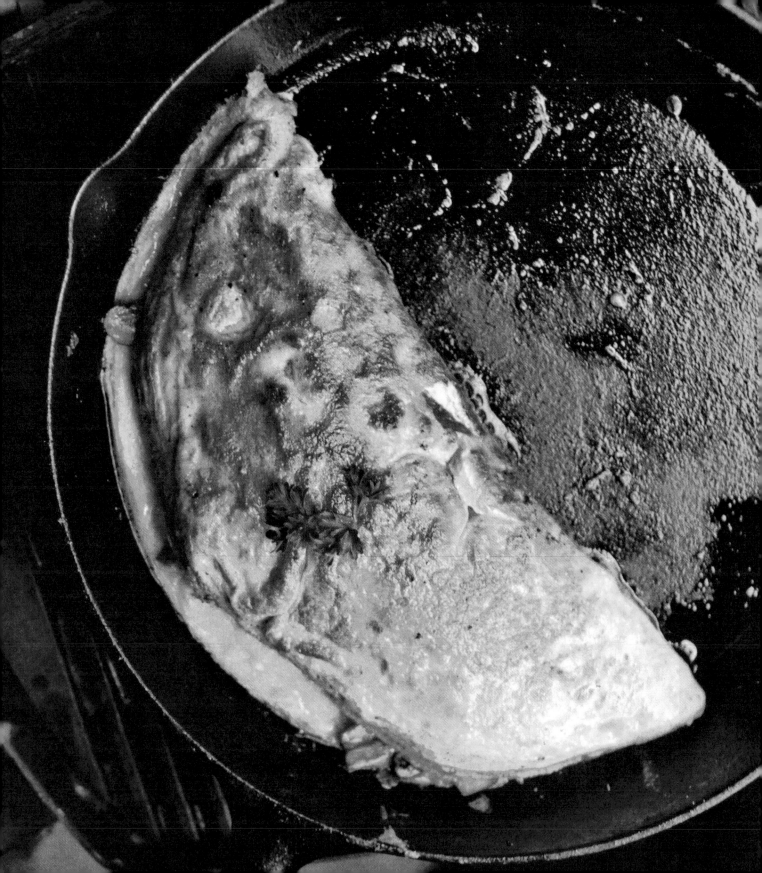

WALLEYE CHEEKY OMELETS
WITH SMOKY BACON & MUSHROOMS

Okay, it's an extravagance, but once a year I like to make an omelet with fish cheeks. They are often the best, smoothest, tastiest part of a fish (or pig or cow). You can make this with smallmouth cheeks, trout cheeks, catfish cheeks . . . it's all good! Once the filling is made, the cooking of the individual omelets goes very quickly.

4 thick slices smoked bacon (4 ounces), cut into ½-inch pieces

¼ pound white mushrooms, thinly sliced

Salt and freshly ground black pepper

3 tablespoons unsalted butter

1 medium onion, chopped

¾ pound walleye cheeks or skinned fillets cut into ½-inch pieces

¼ cup chopped fresh flat-leaf parsley

Hot sauce

12 extra-large eggs

3 tablespoons vegetable oil

2 tablespoons grated Parmesan

SERVES 6

1 In a large skillet, cook the bacon over medium heat until crisp, about 6 minutes. Drain the bacon on paper towels and pour off all but 2 tablespoons of the fat. Add the mushrooms, season with salt and pepper, cover, and cook over medium heat, stirring a few times, until any liquid released by the mushrooms evaporates and the mushrooms brown, about 6 minutes. Add 1 tablespoon of the butter and all the onion and cook until soft, about 5 minutes. Add the walleye, season with salt and pepper, cover, and cook, stirring a few times, until the fish is just cooked, about 3 minutes. Stir in the bacon and parsley and add a few dashes of hot sauce. Cover and set aside.

2 Make each omelet to order: Crack all the eggs in a large bowl and beat with a fork. Season with salt and pepper. Heat an 8-inch nonstick skillet. Add ½ tablespoon of oil and 1 teaspoon of the butter and when the butter stops foaming, add the equivalent of 2 eggs. Cook over medium-high heat, using a heat-proof rubber spatula to push the cooked egg from the edges to the center, while tilting the skillet to allow uncooked egg to pool to the edges. Continue working the eggs, lifting the skillet from the heat to control the cooking, until they are mostly set; this should take only about 30 seconds.

3 Remove the skillet from the heat and smooth out the eggs evenly. Spoon one sixth of the fish filling over half the eggs and sprinkle with 1 teaspoon of the Parmesan. Put the skillet back over the burner on medium-high for a few seconds and shake it lightly to heat and loosen the eggs. Fold the omelet in half and slide onto a warm plate. Repeat with the remaining eggs and filling.

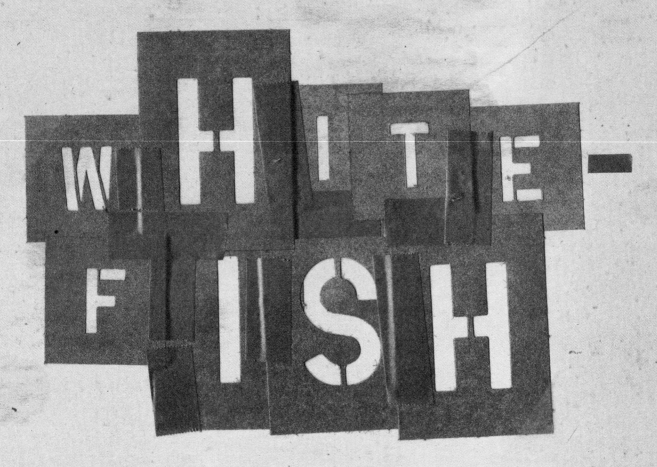

WHITE-FISH

I guess the reason whitefish are called whitefish is that they have white fins. I would be more tempted to call them goldfish (if that name weren't already taken) because they have beautiful golden scales. I've fished for whitefish with rod and reel and, to be truthful, it's not the peak of the angling sport. Netting them with commercial fishermen is a lot more fun, and productive. Whitefish don't get a lot of respect because they are kind of pinheaded. By that I don't mean they are stupid, although I have never given one an I.Q. test. It's just that their head is very small in proportion to their body. Because of this, some old-timers call them humpbacks.

Everywhere you go on lakes Michigan, Huron, and Superior you'll find smokehouses that sell fresh whitefish. The roe is great, too. Once I stopped into a smokehouse in Michigan, bought myself a hard roll and a quarter pound of whitefish, and then, instead of putting mayo on the sandwich, I smeared a couple ounces of whitefish roe on the bread. It gave the sandwich beautiful moistness, smooth texture, and added flavor. In other words, that's everything you'd want in a sandwich without the mayo.

Everyone on the Great Lakes thinks their lake has the best whitefish. Why am I not surprised?

Spring Smoked WHITEFISH CHOWDER
WITH MORELS & RAMPS

It was so nice to be in the Midwest one spring, and I thought it was a shame that the Lake Michigan whitefish didn't have their own chowder. When I think spring, I think morels, asparagus, ramps, and fiddlehead ferns. We have them in New England and they have them in abundance in Michigan, Wisconsin, and Minnesota. You really can't go wrong with those ingredients—and, just for giggles, some chipotle to spice things up. Maybe, someday, some diner in the heartland will do me the honor of calling it Ben's Whitefish Chowder.

1 cup (1 ounce) dried morels, or ½ pound fresh morels, trimmed, halved, and cleaned

4 tablespoons (½ stick) unsalted butter

1 large sweet onion, chopped

Salt and freshly ground black pepper

½ teaspoon smoked sweet paprika

1½ pounds Yukon Gold potatoes, peeled and cut into ½-inch dice

1 quart Fish Stock (page 113) or 2 cups clam juice with 2 cups water

½ pound ramps or scallions, trimmed

½ pound asparagus or fiddlehead ferns, trimmed

½ cup heavy cream

2 large chipotle chiles in adobo, seeded and minced, with 2 teaspoons adobo sauce

2 garlic cloves, minced

½ pound boned and skinned smoked whitefish, torn into large shreds

SERVES 4 TO 6

1 If using dried morels, put them in a medium bowl, cover with 1¼ cups hot water, and let soak until softened, about 10 minutes.

2 Meanwhile, in a large pot, melt 2 tablespoons of the butter. Add the onion, season with salt and pepper, cover, and cook over medium heat, stirring a few times, until softened, about 7 minutes. Stir in the smoked paprika and then add the potatoes. Cook, stirring a few times, until fragrant, about 3 minutes. Add the fish stock and bring to a boil. Partially cover and simmer over low heat until the potatoes are tender, about 10 minutes.

3 Meanwhile, in a medium saucepan, bring 1½ cups of water to a boil. Add a pinch of salt and the ramps and boil over medium-high heat until tender, about 1 minute. With a slotted spoon, transfer the ramps to a medium bowl. Add the asparagus and cook until tender, about 3 minutes. Transfer the asparagus to the bowl. Boil the cooking water until reduced to ¼ cup, about 5 minutes. Pour the reduced water into the pot with the soup. Cut the ramps and asparagus into bite-size pieces.

4   Add the heavy cream to the soup pot and simmer over medium-low heat, stirring a few times and crushing some of the potatoes against the side of the pot, until the chowder is nicely thickened, about 12 minutes. Stir in the chipotles and adobo and reduce the heat to low.

5   If using dried morels, lift them from the soaking water and rinse under running water to remove any grit. Cut the morels crosswise about ½ inch thick. Let the soaking water stand to let grit settle to the bottom. In a large skillet, melt the remaining 2 tablespoons of butter. (If using fresh morels, add them to the skillet, season with salt and pepper, cover, and cook over medium heat, turning once, until browned and tender, about 4 minutes. Add 1 or 2 tablespoons of water if the morels are not yet tender.)

6   Add the morels to the butter, season with salt and pepper, and cook over medium heat until browned and sizzling, about 2 minutes. Add the ramps, asparagus, and garlic and cook, stirring, until the garlic is fragrant and the vegetables are well mixed, about 2 minutes. Scrape the vegetables into the pot. If using, slowly pour the reserved soaking water from the dried morels into the pot, stopping when you reach the grit at the bottom. Simmer the chowder for a few minutes to combine the flavors. Add the whitefish, season with salt and pepper, and warm through.

7   Ladle the chowder into bowls and serve.

The chowder can be refrigerated overnight.

Smoked WHITEFISH PÂTÉ

Many fish pâtés rely on mayonnaise and sour cream. I wanted something with a little more bite to partner with the intense smokiness yet delicate creaminess of smoked whitefish. Crème fraîche and cream cheese work like a charm. This dish is a lifesaver when guests show up, the beers and wine start going down, and people need a little nosh to go along with the drinkies.

1. In a food processor, combine the whitefish, cream cheese, crème fraîche, butter, and wasabi paste, and process until smooth. While processing, scrape down the sides of the processor a few times for even blending.

2. Scrape the pâté into a large bowl, fold in the chives and pepper, and serve with the rye toasts, celery, and endive.

Store the pâté in ½-cup or 1-cup containers in the refrigerator. The pâté can be refrigerated for up to 1 week.

½ pound boned and skinned smoked whitefish, flaked

4 ounces cream cheese, softened

½ cup crème fraîche

4 tablespoons (½ stick) salted butter, softened

1 tablespoon wasabi paste or hot mustard

2 tablespoons minced fresh chives, plus more for garnish

1 teaspoon coarsely cracked black pepper

Rye bread toasts, for serving

Celery sticks and endive spears, for serving

MAKES ABOUT 2½ CUPS; serves 6 to 8

Door County FISH BOIL

Door County, Wisconsin, is a peninsula that sticks out into Lake Michigan and is anchored to the mainland by Green Bay (home of the NFL's Packers). It has the distinction of being the county with the longest coastline in the United States. It's a beautiful, old-timey place famous for its cherries and its whitefish. In the days before the St. Lawrence Seaway, it was also famous for its lake trout, and this recipe is the way the folks up there have adapted to its disappearance. In those bygone days, when the ships had put in and unloaded their catch, they would cut up a few fish they had put aside. Then they would prepare a roaring fire and make a fish boil. They still do it today, and not only for fishermen. Tourists love it, especially the part at the end when the chef pours a force-ten can of kerosene on the fire to produce an enormous flame. The water bubbles out of the pot that the fish is cooking in and takes with it any dirt and fish oil. It's quite a show! Don't worry, no kerosene is required for this stovetop version.

1½ pounds medium red potatoes, scrubbed

8 small onions, peeled, stem ends intact

2 tablespoons kosher salt

8 whitefish steaks, about ½ pound each, or other firm-fleshed fish (lake trout, salmon, or striped bass)

Freshly cracked black pepper

2 tablespoons chopped fresh flat-leaf parsley

6 to 8 tablespoons (¾ to 1 stick) unsalted butter, melted and kept warm

1 lemon, cut into wedges

SERVES 4

1   In a large pot, combine the potatoes, onions, salt, and 2 quarts of water, and bring to a boil over high heat. Partially cover and cook until the potatoes are almost tender, about 15 minutes. Using tongs, place the fish steaks on top of the vegetables. Partially cover the pot again. Reduce the heat to medium and cook the fish until it flakes with a fork, about 10 minutes.

2   Using a slotted spoon, transfer the fish to a warm platter, then place the onions and potatoes alongside. Add cracked black pepper to taste and garnish with the parsley. Serve with melted butter and lemon wedges on the side.

SIDES

BUTTER BEAN CHOWCHOW

Chowchow is a combination of sweet and sour pickled vegetables that is very popular in the American South, although the history books say it arrived there with the Acadians when they left their home in Nova Scotia and settled in Louisiana. I find it is always good to have this on hand to serve with grilled or fried fish. You also can serve large boiled shrimp or smoked fish with chowchow. This chowchow has the addition of butter beans, which make it more substantial as a side dish. It's really great with Catfish Kebabs with Spicy Ketchup Glaze (page 137).

3 quarts apple cider vinegar

1½ cups, packed, light brown sugar

2 tablespoons yellow mustard seeds

2 tablespoons ground turmeric

1 tablespoon celery seeds

1 tablespoon chile flakes

6 green tomatoes, diced

4 red bell peppers, cored, seeded, and diced

2 jalapeños, cored and minced

2 yellow onions, diced

1 small head cabbage, diced

1½ cups butter beans, blanched (boiled until tender and drained)

1 cup yellow mustard

Salt

MAKES ABOUT 4 QUARTS

1 Combine the vinegar and sugar in a large nonreactive pot and heat over medium heat. Reduce by half, then add the mustard seeds, turmeric, celery seeds, and chile flakes. Add the tomatoes, bell and jalapeño peppers, onions, and cabbage. Reduce the heat to low and simmer for 15 minutes or until stewlike. Fold in the blanched butter beans and yellow mustard. Season with salt.

2 Remove from the heat and let cool. Pack into canning jars, cover with lids, and keep refrigerated.

The chowchow can be refrigerated for up to 8 months.

HOT SUMMER SALSA

This is serious salsa—no holding back on the jalapeños. Once you start in on this incredibly fresh-tasting salsa it is impossible to stop eating, so there may not be much left over. Since salt draws liquid from the tomatoes, the salsa is lightly seasoned at first so it won't become too watery. Then just before serving, it is given a final seasoning of salt. The crunchiness of all the vegetables in this salsa would make it a fantastic side dish for the Grilled Gravlax (page 182). Or eat it with the Hot Smoked Bluefish (page 120).

1 pound ripe tomatoes, diced

1 medium onion, diced

4 jalapeños, finely diced, with some seeds

2 tablespoons fresh lime juice

1 teaspoon chili powder

Pinch of sugar

¼ cup chopped fresh cilantro

Salt

MAKES ABOUT 3 CUPS

1 In a large bowl, stir together the tomatoes, onion, jalapeños, lime juice, chili powder, sugar, and cilantro. Season lightly with salt.

2 Cover and refrigerate. Before serving, taste and season with more salt, if needed.

The salsa keeps for 1 or 2 days in the refrigerator.

KALE & CABBAGE SLAW

If you like the crunch of slaw and the way it holds a tangy dressing, but you don't love cabbage, you've kind of been out of luck. In recent years, kale has started to appear in markets and on menus everywhere. This is a good thing. I love kale. Adding it to a slaw recipe tames the cabbage and keeps the crunch. Win-win.

2 cups packed kale leaves (¼ pound), stems removed, leaves chopped

¼ cup fresh lemon juice

Salt and freshly ground black pepper

¼ cup mayonnaise

2 tablespoons ketchup

1 garlic clove, minced

1 tablespoon olive oil

4 cups (½ pound) very thinly sliced cabbage

1 carrot, shredded

SERVES 4 TO 6

1 Put the kale in a large bowl and toss with 2 tablespoons of the lemon juice and a large pinch of salt. Let stand for 15 minutes.

2 In a small bowl, combine the mayonnaise, ketchup, and garlic, then whisk in the remaining 2 tablespoons of lemon juice and all the olive oil. Season with salt and pepper.

3 Add the cabbage and carrot to the bowl of kale and toss. Pour the dressing over and toss well. Cover and refrigerate until chilled.

The slaw can be refrigerated for up to 2 days. Stir well before serving.

SAVOY CABBAGE SLAW WITH CHIPOTLE

Using savoy cabbage here gives the slaw an attractive, more textured appearance. This creamy, spicy slaw can be served alongside simply prepared seafood recipes such as the Crab-Stuffed Roasted Poblanos (page 43), Fried Scallops (page 85), or Grilled Split Lobsters (page 53).

1 cup mayonnaise

2 tablespoons white vinegar

2 tablespoons sugar

1 chipotle chile in adobo, seeded and minced, plus 2 teaspoons adobo sauce

½ tablespoon fresh lime juice

10 cups (1½ pounds) savoy or green cabbage, finely sliced or shredded

Salt and freshly ground black pepper

SERVES 6

In a large bowl, whisk together the mayonnaise, vinegar, sugar, chipotle and adobo, and lime juice. Fold in the cabbage and season with salt and pepper. Cover and refrigerate.

The slaw can be refrigerated for up to 3 days. Stir well before serving.

CUCUMBER SALAD WITH DILL & LIME

Thinly sliced thin-skinned cucumbers, such as Japanese or Armenian, are great for this salad. I like to use a mandoline to slice the cukes. Be sure to use the finger guard so you don't have sliced fingers in your salad, too. You can stack these lime-and-dill-flavored cukes on the Catfish Sandwich with Dill Rémoulade & Sliced Jalapeños (page 135) or the Sardine Sandwich with Fried Eggplant (page 190), or eat them with the Sardine Skewers with Thai Dipping Sauce (page 188).

¾ pound cucumbers, very thinly sliced

Salt and freshly ground black pepper

1½ teaspoons sugar

¼ cup very thinly sliced onion

1 tablespoon cider vinegar

½ teaspoon finely grated lime zest

1 tablespoon fresh lime juice

1 tablespoon olive oil

1 tablespoon chopped fresh dill

SERVES 4 TO 6

1 Put the cucumbers in a large bowl, sprinkle with ½ teaspoon salt and ½ teaspoon of the sugar, and toss well. Refrigerate for 30 minutes.

2 In a small bowl, toss the onion slices with ½ teaspoon of the sugar, ½ tablespoon of the vinegar, and a pinch of salt. Refrigerate for 30 minutes.

3 In a small bowl, combine the remaining ½ teaspoon sugar and ½ tablespoon vinegar along with the lime zest and juice and olive oil. Season with salt and pepper. Combine the onion mixture with the cucumbers and pour the dressing over. Toss well and refrigerate.

4 Just before serving, stir in the dill.

ROASTED MUSHROOMS WITH GARLIC & LEMON

These toasty, smooth-on-the-inside, garlicky 'shrooms are nutty and tangy from the lemon juice. I like them between bites to set up my palate for the next bite. Any sautéed fish benefits from some mushrooms on the side. I love it with the Bacon-Wrapped Grouper Fillets with Lemon-Garlic Relish (page 149) and the Grilled Swordfish with Herbed Beurre Blanc (page 214). I like to add reconstituted tree ears to the mixture once in a while; they are healthy and add crunch.

¼ cup plus 2 tablespoons olive oil

10 large garlic cloves, peeled and quartered

Salt and freshly ground black pepper

1 pound shiitake mushrooms, stems discarded, caps thinly sliced

½ pound white mushrooms, thinly sliced

¼ cup fresh lemon juice

SERVES 6

1 Preheat the oven to 400°F. Put the ¼ cup of olive oil and all the garlic in a large baking dish or cast-iron skillet and season with salt and pepper. Cover with foil and bake for 10 minutes, or until the garlic is soft. Let stand, covered, for 10 minutes.

2 In a large bowl, toss the shiitake and white mushrooms with 3 tablespoons of the lemon juice. Uncover the baking dish and with a fork, mash the garlic. Add the mushrooms and stir well. Add the remaining 2 tablespoons of olive oil and 1 tablespoon of lemon juice, season with salt and pepper, and toss again.

3 Cover and bake for 10 minutes. Uncover the dish and bake for about 30 minutes, until the mushrooms are browned. Stir a few times and serve.

PIGEON PEAS WITH COCONUT MILK & GINGER

Pigeon peas are one of my favorite dried peas, probably because they have such a cute name. In Puerto Rico and many areas in the Caribbean, pigeon peas, or gunga peas, are an important part of any meal. Many folks like to use the canned green variety, which is slightly different from the easier-to-find dried brown peas used here. This side dish is substantial, but most importantly for a side, it is richly flavored.

2 cups dried pigeon peas
(¾ pound)

Salt

2 tablespoons vegetable oil

1 medium onion, diced

2 garlic cloves, minced

2 teaspoons chopped fresh thyme

2 teaspoons grated peeled fresh ginger

2 jalapeños, minced, with some seeds

1 tablespoon tomato paste

1 cup unsweetened coconut milk

½ cup chicken stock

3 tablespoons chopped fresh cilantro

SERVES 6

1. Put the peas in a large pot and cover with water by 2 inches. Bring to a boil, cover, and remove from the heat. Let stand for 1 hour.

2. Uncover and bring back to a boil. Add more water to maintain the 2-inch level and simmer over medium-low heat, stirring a few times, until tender, about 40 minutes. Stir in 1 tablespoon salt and remove from the heat. Let stand for 5 minutes and drain.

3. In a large pot, heat the oil. Add the onion, garlic, thyme, ginger, and jalapeños and cook over medium heat until softened, about 8 minutes. Stir in the tomato paste. Add the coconut milk and stock and bring to a simmer. Add the peas and stir well. Cover and simmer over medium-low heat for 20 minutes, or until thick and stewlike. Season with salt, stir in the cilantro, and serve.

The peas can be refrigerated for up to 2 days.

GRILLED CORN SALSA

The corn here is grilled in the husk to keep it moist and help it steam while grilling. It is then given another round on the grill, after it is shucked, to char the kernels for a smoky taste. It is a terrific addition to the Snakehead Chimichurri Tacos (page 197) but will liven up and add spicy crunch to any number of dishes such as Reddened Blackfish (page 115), Hot Smoked Bluefish (page 120), or Grilled Whole Porgies with Smoky Tomato Chutney (page 173).

2 large ears corn, outer leaves shucked, a thin layer of leaves left on

1 tablespoon olive oil, plus more for brushing

Salt and freshly ground black pepper

½ cup finely diced onion

1 jalapeño, seeded and minced

3 tablespoons fresh lime juice

3 tablespoons chopped fresh cilantro

MAKES 2 CUPS

1. Prepare the salsa: Light a grill. Put the ears of corn on the grill over medium heat, cover, and grill, turning, until charred all over but still tender in the middle, about 25 minutes. It's fine if the leaves burn at the ends. Hold the ends of the ears of corn with tongs and while using a kitchen towel, peel the leaves from the corn back to the stem. Brush the corn with olive oil and grill over high heat, turning, until browned in spots, about 10 minutes.

2. Season the corn with salt and pepper and let cool to warm. Working over a large bowl, cut the kernels from the cobs into the bowl. With a fork, break up the kernels. Stir in the onion, jalapeño, lime juice, cilantro, and the 1 tablespoon of olive oil. Season with salt and pepper and serve or refrigerate and serve lightly chilled.

The salsa can be refrigerated for up to 3 days. Serve at room temperature or lightly chilled.

CREAMED CORN

Creamed corn can be the basis for a chowder or served as a side to just about anything, especially crispy, fried fish. I wait until the corn is at its peak and supersweet. Fresh-picked corn makes all the difference.

2 tablespoons unsalted butter

1 medium sweet onion, finely diced

Salt

5 ears corn, shucked, kernels cut from the cobs, all juices reserved

½ teaspoon turmeric

½ teaspoon sugar

2 tablespoons fine yellow cornmeal

½ cup heavy cream

SERVES 4

1. In a large skillet, melt the butter. Add the onion and a pinch of salt and cook over medium-low heat, stirring a few times, until softened, about 8 minutes. Add the corn kernels and juices, cover, and cook, stirring a few times, until the corn is just tender, about 5 minutes.

2. Uncover the skillet, add the turmeric and sugar, and cook, stirring, until fragrant, about 1 minute. Stir in the cornmeal, then slowly stir in the cream until smooth. Simmer over low heat, stirring a few times, until the mixture is thickened, about 3 minutes. Season with salt and serve.

The creamed corn can be refrigerated for up to 2 days. Reheat gently.

HUSH PUPPIES

You can't have a proper fish fry without hush puppies. But you can have hush puppies with anything you like: barbecued ribs, pulled pork, smoked brisket. Oh yeah, this is a seafood cookbook. Well, how about beautiful king salmon fillets in season? Or grilled lobsters? Hey, hush puppies are fried, salty, and savory; that means they can pretty much go with everything.

¾ cup all-purpose flour

¾ cup fine cornmeal

1½ tablespoons sugar

2½ teaspoons baking soda

1½ teaspoons kosher salt

¾ teaspoon cayenne pepper

½ teaspoon freshly ground black pepper

2 scallions, chopped

2 large eggs

¾ cup whole milk

Vegetable oil, for frying

Tartar sauce or rémoulade sauce, for serving (optional)

MAKES ABOUT 30

1 In a large bowl, whisk together the flour, cornmeal, sugar, baking soda, salt, cayenne, black pepper, and scallions.

2 In a smaller bowl, whisk the eggs, then whisk in the milk. Fold the egg mixture into the flour mixture.

3 In a large saucepan, heat 1½ inches of vegetable oil to 325°F. Have a rack set over a large rimmed baking sheet near the stove. Drop level tablespoons of the batter into the hot oil, frying 6 hush puppies at a time. Fry, turning a few times, until browned and crisp, about 2 minutes. With a slotted spoon, drain the hush puppies on the rack and repeat with the remaining batter. Serve hot with the tartar or rémoulade sauce, if using.

CUBAN YELLOW RICE

Rice is an important part of almost any meal in the Caribbean. This simple, authentic rice dish is meant to accompany a large family meal to soak up sauce. It calls for achiote, also known as annatto, which is the seed of a tropical plant. The orange seed is used in cooking for the vibrant color that it gives to a recipe.

1 tablespoon vegetable oil

½ small onion, minced

½ teaspoon ground achiote or annatto

2 cups long-grain rice, rinsed and drained

1 bay leaf

2 teaspoons salt

SERVES 6

1 In a 3-quart saucepan, heat the oil. Add the onion and cook over medium heat until softened, about 4 minutes. Add the achiote and cook, stirring, about 20 seconds. Add the rice, 4½ cups of water, the bay leaf, and salt and stir. Bring the water to a boil, cover, and cook over low heat until the water has been absorbed and the rice is tender, about 15 minutes.

2 Keep the rice covered and remove from the burner. Let stand for 10 minutes. Lift the lid and wipe the underside of it with a paper towel so the condensation doesn't drip into the rice. Lightly fluff the rice, discard the bay leaf, cover, and let stand for up to 25 minutes before serving.

CREAMED SPINACH

Has there ever been a fish house or chop house that didn't serve creamed spinach? You can throw in steak houses, too. Instead of adding flour to thicken the spinach—which does zero for flavor—I add body and richness with Parmesan cheese. Righteous spinach! One of my all-time-favorite simple dinners is grilled fish served with creamed spinach and Whole Smashed Potatoes with Cream (below). Often my fish of choice is bluefish or swordfish. Try this spinach with the Whole Bluefish in Foil (page 124) or with Grilled Split Lobsters (page 53).

1 pound spinach, long stems removed

1 cup heavy cream

2 garlic cloves, minced

⅛ teaspoon cayenne pepper

⅛ teaspoon freshly grated nutmeg

½ cup grated Parmesan or Pecorino

Salt and freshly ground black pepper

SERVES 4

1 In a large pot, bring ½ inch of water to a boil. Add half the spinach and cook, stirring until wilted, about 1 minute. With a slotted spoon, transfer the spinach to a colander and repeat with the remaining spinach. When cool, squeeze out the water from the spinach and chop it.

2 Wipe out the pot and add the cream and garlic. Bring to a boil and simmer over medium heat until reduced by half, about 3 minutes. Add the cayenne and nutmeg and remove the pot from the heat. Add the spinach and stir well. Cook over low heat, stirring often, until the spinach is simmering, about 2 minutes. Remove from the heat and stir in the cheese. Season with salt and pepper and serve.

WHOLE SMASHED POTATOES WITH CREAM

Don't let me forget mashed potatoes. I never do when I'm cooking. Good ol' creamed and butter-mashed potatoes are wonderful, but garlic makes them heavenly. The pairing of fish and potatoes is a beautiful thing.

1½ pounds baby Yukon Gold potatoes, scrubbed

Salt and freshly ground black pepper

2 tablespoons unsalted butter, at room temperature

1 cup heavy cream, warmed

2 garlic cloves, minced

SERVES 4 TO 6

1 Put the potatoes in a large saucepan and cover with water. Bring to a boil, add a large pinch of salt, and boil over medium-high heat until tender, about 12 minutes. Drain the potatoes and add back to the pan. Shake the potatoes over the hot burner for about 10 seconds to dry them, then remove from the burner.

2 Add the butter and, with a potato masher, mash the potatoes coarsely. Add the cream and garlic and mash well. Season with salt and pepper and serve.

BUTTER-BAKED POTATOES

This is a simple but incredibly delicious way to make buttery and crisp potatoes. It's all in the method. You boil the potatoes first, coat them with butter, and let them bake a good long time. You can use a melon baller and cut out little potato balls if you want. For breakfast, serve these alongside the Walleye Cheeky Omelets with Smoky Bacon & Mushrooms (page 227), or try them instead of rice with the Baby Squid Sauté with Green Garlic Sauce (page 106).

3 pounds Yukon Gold potatoes, peeled and cut into 1-inch dice

5 tablespoons unsalted butter, melted

Salt and freshly ground black pepper

SERVES 6

1 Preheat the oven to 400°F. Put the potatoes in a large pot, cover with water, and bring to a boil over medium-high heat. Cook until they are just tender but still hold their shape, about 7 minutes. Drain the potatoes well and put them on a large rimmed baking sheet in an even layer. Let them air dry for about 10 minutes.

2 Pour the melted butter over the potatoes and toss to coat thoroughly. Arrange the potatoes evenly and season with salt and pepper. Bake for about 30 minutes, until golden brown and sizzling, and then serve.

SEA BISCUITS

1¾ cups all-purpose flour

½ teaspoon salt

2 teaspoons baking powder

½ teaspoon sugar

½ teaspoon baking soda

5 tablespoons unsalted butter, cut into small pieces and chilled

¾ cup buttermilk

1 extra-large egg mixed with 1 teaspoon milk for egg wash

Coarse salt and coarsely cracked black pepper

MAKES ABOUT 20 BISCUITS

Sea Biscuits can be rock-hard (mine aren't) and they last a long time, which is why they were the go-to ration for generations of sailors. Mine are based on the way these evolved in New England into flaky but sturdy salt-and-pepper biscuits. They are perfect for dunking into chowder or dipping into smoky fish dip.

1 In a large bowl, combine the flour, salt, baking powder, sugar, and baking soda. With a pastry cutter, cut in the butter quickly until the mixture resembles coarse meal. Pour in the buttermilk and mix until a smooth dough forms. Do not overwork the dough.

2 Preheat the oven to 450°F. Line 2 large baking sheets with parchment paper. On a lightly floured work surface, roll the dough to ¼ inch thickness and cut with a floured 2-inch-round biscuit cutter. Place the biscuits on the baking sheets. Brush the biscuits with the egg wash and top each with a sprinkling of coarse salt and coarsely cracked pepper.

3 Bake on the lower and middle racks for 12 minutes, rotating the pans top to bottom and front to back one time during baking. Serve warm or at room temperature.

The biscuits can be stored in an airtight container for up to 5 days.

FRENCH BREAD BOWLS

What's more fun than eating your chowder in a crusty bread bowl and then eating the bowl? Nothing that I can think of. Break off the top of the bowl and dip the pieces in the chowder as you eat. Or, if that is too adventuresome for you, just make the rolls and serve alongside, and dip as you go. You'll need six ¾-cup ramekins, 3½ inches across.

1 package active dry yeast

⅓ cup warm water

¼ teaspoon sugar

1 cup cold water

3½ cups all-purpose flour, plus more for dusting

1¾ teaspoons salt

Soft butter, for the ramekins

MAKES 6 BOWLS OR 12 ROLLS

1 In a medium bowl, combine the yeast with the warm water and sugar. Let stand until foamy, about 4 minutes. Stir in the cold water.

2 In a heavy-duty standing mixer fitted with the dough hook, combine the flour, salt, and yeast mixture. Mix on low for 1 minute. Then let the dough rest for 5 minutes. Place the dough on a floured work surface and knead for 5 minutes, or until smooth and elastic. Place the dough back in the mixer bowl (no need to clean or oil), cover, and let rise for 1 hour.

3 On a lightly floured work surface, knead the dough by flattening it and folding it in thirds, 3 times. Place the dough back in the same bowl, cover, and let rise until it triples in volume, approximately 1½ hours.

4 Preheat the oven to 450°F. Lightly flour the work surface and cut the dough into 6 equal pieces. Roll each piece into a 5-inch circle. Butter the bottom and sides of the outside of the ramekins, then place them upside down on 2 rimmed baking sheets. Gently drape the dough rounds over the upside-down ramekins. Bake for 20 minutes, switching the baking sheets top to bottom and back to front one time.

5 Remove from the oven and lift the bread bowls from the ramekins. Place the breads back on the baking sheets and in the oven, open side up, for about 10 minutes. Remove from the oven and cool on a rack.

6 As an alternative, to make the rolls, cut the dough into 12 equal pieces. Gently stretch the sides of each piece underneath to the bottom, forming little balls, so there's an unbroken skin all around, with the seam on the bottom. Cover with a large, wide bowl or plastic wrap and let rise for 45 minutes to 1 hour. Put the rolls on a lightly oiled baking sheet and bake at 450°F for about 20 minutes, until golden.

ACKNOWLEDGMENTS

This is amazing! So many people helped me on this book. It's almost impossible to thank everybody! You see, I was never a good student growing up. In fact, I had a lot of trouble reading and writing in my early years. So, I find it a little ironic and very exciting that a dyslexic kid like me would one day grow up to have his very own book! I have a lot of very special people to thank for having believed in me along the way . . . and most of them would agree, it's almost a miracle!

I have my mom to thank, first and foremost, which is why this book is dedicated to her. She believed in me the most, and I only wish she were around now so we could cook together.

Paul: You are the best stepfather any kid/grown-up could ever ask for! You have also brought into my life the best brothers and sisters anyone could ever ask for.

My dad, Bill: You really are the person I have to thank for introducing me to nature, the sea, and fish. You are a scientist, a naturalist, and real wonder. It is just amazing to hear you talk about a single tide pool!

My grandfather, Pup: You taught me how to fish. Pup, thank you for picking me as your fishing buddy. Fishing with you was one of the best experiences a kid could ever have.

My teachers: You believed in me and took it upon yourselves to teach me some impossible things. Wow, how sorry I feel for all of you having to put up with me. Watching me do algebra was like watching some people try to parallel park.

Peter Kaminsky: You're a fine fisherman and a wonderful writer and chef. You gave me lots of advice on the writing of this book long before I mustered up the courage to ask you to help me write it! Thanks, Peter, for listening to all my stories and for guiding me through this process.

Annica: Thank you for holding on to every photo, drawing, scrap, and graphic we have ever done together. None of this would have been possible without you. You're the best designer ever!

My editor, Emily Takoudes: You believed in this book from the get-go. Thank you for all your excitement and hard work.

Danny: Thank you for having sat with me in the early stages, and for hashing out ideas and coming up with a concept. And just for believing in me overall.

Gabi: Thank you for your AMAZING eye! I knew I wanted to work with you long before you even knew I was checking out your work. Thanks for putting up with me.

Marcia: Thank you for the testing and retesting and testing again. You are a force and a seafood lover and a wonderful chef.

Lauren: Thank you for understanding how artists think.

Luke: Thank you for putting up with me when I bullied you.

Kasia Cyle: Thank you for your help and patience.

Michael: Thank you for putting up with me on early fishing adventures. Sorry for torturing you with eels and lobster.

The Dewees/Blaut family: Thank you for letting me make huge messes in the kitchen and for being my recipe testers!

Greta, Leah, and Luke: So many fun dinners with all you guys. Miss those!

H, L, and D team: Thank you for all our amazing adventures. What a blast!

Steve Troha: Thank you for making this entire book happen! You believed in it from the start.

Cody Raisig, Christina Kim, and anyone who took a cool shot for this book at some point: Thanks to all of you!

Paul: Thank you for introducing me to grilling in the freezing cold in Vermont!

My dog, Fletcher: Thank you for joining me on all my adventures.

Adam: You believed in me and helped me along the way.

The Sargent family: Thank you for your love of the outdoors.

The Feinberg family: I thank you for your love of family.

All my brothers and sisters: Thank you for the adventures!

My wonderful fishing and surfing friends: You make being on the water such a pleasure!

Finally, thank you to the fish . . . I love fish. You are beautiful creatures and I want you around forever!

INDEX

Thank You!